A Beginner's Guide to Prayer

Augsburg Beginner's Guides introduce readers to key subjects in the past and present of the Christian tradition. Beginner's Guides strive to be readable and yet reliable, simply written but not simplistic in their approach. Each book in the series includes the information that is needed for an overview of the subject and as a solid foundation for further study.

A Beginner's Guide to Reading the Bible
   by Craig R. Koester

A Beginner's Guide to the Books of the Bible
   by Diane L. Jacobson and Robert Kysar

A Beginner's Guide to Studying the Bible
   by Rolf E. Aaseng

A Beginner's Guide to Prayer
   by Richard J. Beckmen

A Beginner's Guide to
PRAYER

Richard J. Beckmen

MINNEAPOLIS

A BEGINNER'S GUIDE TO PRAYER

Cover design and illustration: Catherine Reishus McLaughlin

Library of Congress Cataloging-in-Publication Data

Beckmen, Richard J.
   A beginner's guide to prayer / Richard J. Beckmen.
     p.   cm.
   Includes bibliographical references.
   ISBN 0-8066-2674-7 (alk. paper) :
    1. Prayer—Christianity.   I. Title.
   BV210.2.B39   1994
   248.3'2—dc20   94-1577
                                              CIP

Manufactured in the U.S.A.   AF 9-2674

98   97   96   3   4   5   6   7   8   9   10

Contents

The Cry for Mercy
The Cry of Abandonment

Author's Preface

This book is a small contribution to a very large subject. In this volume you will encounter a broad introduction to prayer, its forms, its obstacles, its promises, and its questions.

The thoughts of many teachers, friends, and companions on the prayer journeys are a part of this book. I am grateful to all who have shared in the writing of this book—my wife and daily prayer companion, Solveig; my children Kari, Siri, John, and Mikkel for whom I have prayed every day in order to accompany their life journey; and several congregations in which I was nurtured into a spirit of prayer.

Most of all I am grateful to God whose soft voice made it clear that I was created and loved in order to pray. I am grateful to the Holy Spirit who convinced me of the necessity of prayer, and God's divine Wisdom who taught me the joy of prayer.

This beginner's guide is for all of us, because God is always teaching us new lessons in prayer. The compelling truth that God desires and delights in the conversation we call prayer should be encouragement enough for each of us eagerly to pursue our end of the conversation.

1

Introduction to Prayer

There is no single reason why you may be drawn to pray. You may feel like a victim of circumstances beyond your control. You reach out beyond yourself and other humans to touch the edge of eternity, hoping to find divine power to intercede and deliver you.

Memories of a childhood intimacy with God now absent in the rush of a busy life may draw you to seek prayer in order to restore a relationship with God that once seemed so close and comforting.

A man sitting next to me on the plane noticed I was reading a book about God. He started a conversation that soon got around to the story of his life, especially as it related to God. Before the flight was over he had shared with me the tale of his loss of intimacy with God. He no longer prayed, and he was not even sure how to begin. He began asking me to tell him how to recapture that close communication with God.

Grief, too, may kindle in you a desire to learn to pray. The loss of a loved one in death, divorce, separation, or abandonment pushes one to the edge. In desperation you may turn to God.

You may turn to prayer because you are called from within to explore the inner world of your being, your soul.

In whatever way God may catch their attention, humans are moved to pray, or at least to begin asking the questions that can lead to prayer.

Where is the caring One who hears, listens, and responds to my needs?

Where is the One who loves me deeply so that my need for intimacy is satisfied?

Where is the One in whose presence joy erupts from my heart?

Where is the One who understands my pain and frustration?

These are questions that have their roots in the search for spirituality—the discovery of a relationship that nurtures the deepest part of us.

Of course there are some who have prayed their entire lives. Those who have been involved in Twelve-Step groups speak of their experience in discovering that the deepest and primary issue in facing and sustaining freedom from addictive behavior is their spirituality, a surrendered relationship to a power greater than themselves.

C. G. Jung, who served as psychiatrist to many, said that all his patients ultimately were faced with spiritual issues.

The great theologian Augustine exclaimed, "Our hearts are restless until they find their rest in you, O God."

Ultimately the act of prayer does not come from within ourselves alone. In many ways God is the initiator of prayer. Prayer is the response to an invitation that comes from God to be part of a loving relationship with the One who made us, sustains us, and finally saves us from ourselves and the power of sin to destroy us.

Jesus' invitation to prayer is seen in the wonderful way in which he elicits responses from people who are in need. Coming upon a man who was blind on his way into Jericho, Jesus has the man brought to him when he cries out for mercy. The man's cry is a prayer that rises out of his need, but he must already have heard of this gracious, powerful healer who had come to town. When the man appears, Jesus asks him a simple question: "What do you want me to do for you?" This open-ended question is an invitation to the man who was blind to allow his imagination and need to come together in a creative response to the compassion and grace offered in the question. We can imagine the anticipated joy in his face and the sound of humility in his voice as he says, "Lord, let me see again" (Luke 18:41).

The amazing thing about prayer is that God is always there, even before we think of praying. God already calls and invites us to experience a relationship in which the divine can touch our lives. God creates the foundation of the relationship and the desire within us to enter into it.

The prophet Isaiah reminds us that God is aware and responsive even before we can utter our prayer. "Before they call I will answer, while they are yet speaking I will hear" (Isa. 65:24).

Scripture provides a view of God's heart that reaches out to invite our prayers, especially in the ministry of Jesus who seeks to draw out the desires of our heart into the open so that God's love and grace can operate in our life.

Does Prayer Work?

Is God experienced today as more than a spectator to my life journey?

In this book you are invited to explore various descriptions of prayer that come from the conviction that "prayer is the mightiest force in the world," and that it provides an avenue for a spirituality that can speak to the deepest yearnings and searchings of the human heart today.

Does prayer work? It is important to explore what this question might mean and how it can be answered.

What do we mean by the word *work*? If it means we can run an experiment such as we might do in a laboratory, then the answer would be no. Scientific thinking that is based on a cause-and-effect relationship that is always repeatable will not work in relation to prayer. This would assume that we can control the mind and activity of God by some means that will ensure that God will do whatever we ask. There really is no formula that will guarantee a prayer being answered in the way we want it to be answered.

If by asking, Does prayer work? we mean, Does God hear our prayer and answer according to his will and purpose? the answer is yes.

There is an important assumption that lies beneath this question. The assumption has to do with who is in charge and how we understand the world and ourselves in relationship to God.

Our natural inclination is to believe that our life is the center of the universe. All others, including God, revolve about our life.

11

Imagine the thinking of people before the time of Galileo. They believed that the sun, moon, stars, and planets revolved about the earth. Everything else, it was believed, moved according to a plan that served earth. We now know that the sun is at the center of our world and all else revolves about it. This image may illumine our relationship to God and the purpose of life. I may believe that my will, understanding, and feelings are at the center of my existence, and all else is to serve me, including God. However, the biblical picture has God at the center, while my life and the lives of others are meant to orbit around the will and purpose of God.

This transformation involves moving the center of your life from your ego, that self-conscious controlling center, to that spiritual center within yourself where God directs your life. The apostle Paul describes his own experience of the transformation in Galatians 2:19-20:

> For through the law I died to the law, so that I might live to God. I have been crucified with Christ; and it is no longer I who live, but it is Christ who lives in me. And the life I now live in the flesh I live by faith in the Son of God, who loved me and gave himself for me.

Effective prayer is an expression of a transformed relationship with a living and personal God.

Does prayer work? If your relationship with God is working, prayer is working. This is rooted in the fact that we are to have an "I-Thou" relationship with God rather than an "I-it" relationship. God is not an impersonal force, a statistical mathematical formula, or an automatic vending machine. God is alive and personal, and God interacts through relationships.

Prayer and Your Relationship to God

It is important to understand the relationship into which you are called with God. What you think of God will greatly affect how and why you pray. If your God is too small, you may end up thinking you will have to do most things yourself. If your God is too miserly, you may not have any great expectations. If your

God is too much like yourself, you may feel disillusioned. If your God is too much like a salesperson, you may end up always bargaining. If your God is angry, you will probably try to hide out. None of these images carries a positive or accurate picture of God.

In John 15, Jesus describes the nature of the relationship between God and the believer: it is initiated, sustained, and interpreted through the person of Jesus. This is a critical issue for Christians.

Our relationship to God is mediated through Jesus Christ. That is, we understand who God is through the teachings and actions of Jesus. On our part, we present ourselves to God in Jesus Christ.

Two passages from John 15 will be examined to see what Jesus taught about prayer and relationship. Read John 15:1-11 and notice the way in which prayer is linked to your relationship with Christ.

I am the true vine, and my Father is the vinegrower. He removes every branch in me that bears no fruit. Every branch that bears fruit he prunes to make it bear more fruit. You have already been cleansed by the word that I have spoken to you. Abide in me as I abide in you. Just as the branch cannot bear fruit by itself unless it abides in the vine, neither can you unless you abide in me. I am the vine, you are the branches. Those who abide in me and I in them bear much fruit, because apart from me you can do nothing. Whoever does not abide in me is thrown away like a branch and withers; such branches are gathered, thrown into the fire, and burned. If you abide in me, and my words abide in you, ask for whatever you wish, and it will be done for you. My Father is glorified by this, that you bear much fruit and become my disciples. As the Father has loved me, so I have loved you; abide in my love. If you keep my commandments, you will abide in my love, just as I have kept my Father's commandments and abide in his love. I have said these things to you so that my joy may be in you, and that your joy may be complete.

You can notice several aspects of the relationship Jesus is describing. First, the image of the vine and branches describes an organic nature to the relationship. It is alive, real, and interdependent. The branches cannot live without nourishment from the vine. The vine depends on the branches to bear fruit.

Secondly, the word *abide* conveys a sense of intimacy in the relationship. It denotes being at home or dwelling within. In addition, the relationship is marked by love, obedience, and discipline.

Out of this kind of relationship with Christ prayer flows naturally and comfortably. To pray is not foreign or alien to your life as a Christian. It is the way you respond to this mutual abiding, you in Christ and Christ's word in you (v. 7). This relationship allows you freedom and expectation to request of God what you wish. This implies that because of this relationship with Christ you will know how and for what to pray.

Jesus also teaches in this passage that you can be identified in him as he is in the Father (vv. 9-10). Therefore, you are a child of God and can ask as a child asks of a father. Similar thoughts are written by the apostle Paul in Galatians 4:4-6:

But when the fullness of time had come, God sent his Son, born of a woman, born under the law, in order to redeem those who were under the law, so that we might receive adoption as children. And because you are children, God has sent the Spirit of his Son into our hearts, crying, "Abba! Father!"

In John's Gospel, Jesus continues his teaching about the relationship that is established and allows us to pray with confidence and without fear:

This is my commandment, that you love one another as I have loved you. No one has greater love than this, to lay down one's life for one's friends. You are my friends if you do what I command you. I do not call you servants any longer, because the servant does not know what the master is doing; but I have called you friends, because I have made known to you everything that I have heard from my Father. You did not choose me but I chose you. And I appointed you to go and bear fruit, fruit that will last, so that the Father will give you whatever you ask him in my name. (John 15:12-16)

When you pray out of this type of relationship with Christ, you are not standing on the outside looking in. You are on the inside, sharing in the love and friendship of Christ as a child of God. Notice in these verses how Christ includes you as a friend in the inner circle of knowledge and the inner circle of his love. Notice, also, how you have been chosen and appointed to bear fruit. You belong.

This may be difficult for you to accept. Grace is difficult to accept. You may be conscious of your shortcomings and feel quite inadequate to claim such a stature before God.

Yet, there it is. In Christ you are a chosen, loved, and sent child of God. And being in Christ, you can ask whatever you will in Jesus' name (v. 16).

Christians pray in Jesus' name. However, it is not used as some sort of magical phrase like "Open, Sesame!" from the story of "Ali Baba and the Forty Thieves." It is used because your relationship with God has been established through Jesus Christ and rests on your continuing relationship to him.

God has closed the distance between himself and you in Christ. In Christ God has claimed you as a child. As a child of God in Christ, you have a child's rights and privileges from a parent.

This means that you do not have to talk God into loving you or hearing your prayer. You do not have to bargain with God in prayer, haggling as if you were dealing with a merchant in the marketplace. You simply ask because of the kind of relationship you now have with God in Jesus Christ. Jesus' name and your willingness to identify with it provide the basis for your prayer.

Prayer as Primary Activity of Religious Life

Some people think prayer is "saying a prayer"—speaking a particular intention to God. However, prayer can be understood as more general than that. Prayer in a broad sense links all aspects of your life to God.

In our culture a dominant way of thinking says that life can be divided into sacred times and secular times, sacred activities and secular activities. God is allowed to be present only at designated moments. The rest of the time God is put away and life is lived under our own control.

15

Prayer can be used in this way. We can set aside certain times and certain places to pray and omit prayer from the rest of our life.

The Bible teaches us to think a different way. God is present in all of life. We may set aside certain times and places for worship, but God is not absent at any time or in any place. It is right and proper to pray at all times and in all places.

Prayer is the name we give to the experience of being in communication with God wherever we are and in whatever we are doing.

Prayer is experience because it involves our senses, minds, souls, and spirits. When we pray we know that it is happening. Prayer is a point of interaction with God.

Prayer is communication because it involves giving and receiving. It is sharing between two living, personal beings—God and yourself. In all the various forms and methods of prayer, there is something going on between the person of the Christian and the person of God.

You are sharing your life—your needs, feelings, concerns, and desires. God is responding with divine presence, consolation, insight, and change.

To be sure, this is not communication between equals. As Creator, Divine Spirit, God is far above and beyond that which we can know. God has revealed in Jesus much of God's heart, will, and mind. However, we acknowledge that we do not know all there is to know about God.

We know God's name, and we know the mystery of his will in Christ Jesus to draw all persons to himself. We know God's continuing presence in the Holy Spirit and all of the ways the Holy Spirit ministers in our lives. This tension between our knowing and our not knowing about God affects our prayer life. This tension between God's otherness and our likeness to God, our being created in God's image, defines some of the struggle in prayer.

God remains in control but is open to our requests and intercessions. God remains essentially hidden yet gives glimpses of his workings and will. God is holy and other from us yet dwells among us and in us through the Holy Spirit. God is distant yet near. Our own condition adds to the dilemma created by the differences between God and ourselves. We are limited to space

16

and time yet are touched by the eternal. We are sinners, yet through Christ's redemption we are invited to the throne room of God. We stumble in darkness, yet God shares light and revelation with us. Our trust in God is tainted by shame, fear, and guilt, yet God desires that we come close to him as he has come close to us.

All of these tensions say that prayer needs to be grounded in humility but expressed in faith and hope.

Most of Jesus' teaching on prayer focuses on this basic point. Pray as a child to a parent. Pray as a creature to the divine Creator. Pray as a sinner to the Holy One. But, at the same time pray as a friend of God. Pray in confidence that God hears and will respond. Pray persistently and fervently because your prayers make a difference. Pray in humility as the earth creature that you are, but pray with all confidence and hope as the beloved child of God that you are.

Prayer, broadly understood, is also the way in which we offer all of who we are and what we do in the dialogue with God. Our spirituality is a part of our body, mind, feelings, and will. It is a part of our worship, work, play, and rest. As God seeks to be always and everywhere present, so we seek to be always and everywhere present to God.

This way of understanding prayer was a particular tradition in Celtic spirituality and is expressed in this prayer of St. Patrick:

At Tara today, the strength of God pilot me, the power of God preserve me. May the wisdom of God instruct me, the eye of God watch over me, the ear of God hear me, the word of God give me sweet talk, the hand of God defend me, the way of God guide me.
Christ be with me.
Christ before me.
Christ after me.
Christ in me.
Christ under me.
Christ over me.
Christ on my right hand.
Christ on my left hand.
Christ on this side.
Christ on that side.

17

Christ at my back.
Christ in the head of everyone to whom I speak.
Christ in the mouth of every person who speaks to me.
Christ in the eye of every person who looks upon me.
Christ in the ear of everyone who hears me at Tara today.
Amen.

Prayer is centering your life in the spiritual relationship with God in Christ and allowing that center to be present in all that you do.

Christ will satisfy the hungering soul. Christ will bring solace to the pained heart. Christ will respond to the cry for mercy or the complaint for justice. Christ will be there when you simply need to feel that your relationship with God is warm and real. Christ will be there for rest, guidance, joy, love, and hope.

Prayer is the presenting of your whole life and the lives of others to God, so that God may be known and lives may be touched by grace.

Prayer and the Holy Spirit

The substance of your relationship with God, as described above, is provided by Jesus Christ. In Christ, God's love, grace, and desire to draw you near are made possible.

The Holy Spirit, on the other hand, is the energy of your relationship with God. The Holy Spirit is the dynamic presence of God given to you to know and trust with confidence the relationship that God establishes with you in Christ.

The Holy Spirit is the "present tense" of God. The Spirit makes real in your life what Jesus spoke long ago—serving the purposes of God to bring Jesus' teaching and work into the present moment.

Jesus promised an intimate relationship with God based upon his death and resurrection. This relationship is established in baptism and continues to be lived out in faith.

Do you not know that all of us who have been baptized into Christ Jesus were baptized into his death? Therefore we have been buried with him by baptism into death, so that, just as Christ was raised from the dead by the glory of the Father, so we too might walk in newness of life. (Rom. 6:3-4)

18

The Holy Spirit, given in baptism, is God's continuing presence at work through all of your life's ages and stages.

The apostle Paul describes the role of the Holy Spirit in sustaining your relationship as God's child:

> For all who are led by the Spirit of God are children of God. For you did not receive a spirit of slavery to fall back into fear, but you have received a spirit of adoption. When we cry, "Abba! Father!" it is that very Spirit bearing witness with our spirit that we are children of God. (Rom. 8:14-16)

Paul also warns against "grieving the Spirit" (Eph. 4:30) or "quenching the Spirit" (1 Thess. 5:19). To do either of these is to hinder the Spirit's work of nurturing you in the new life. If you distance yourself from the Spirit through neglect or resistance, your relationship with God will be only something remembered from the past but not experienced now.

If the Spirit is ignored, your prayer life will suffer along with other aspects of your faith life. In a stirring passage about maintaining a strong spiritual life in the face of spiritual enemies, Paul includes constant prayer in the Spirit as one of the components necessary to ensure survival (Eph. 6:10-18).

When you are neither able nor conscious of what you should pray about, the Holy Spirit is also present in you to pray. A very comforting passage from Paul describes how the Spirit will pray in you even when all you can do is groan:

> Likewise the Spirit helps us in our weakness; for we do not know how to pray as we ought, but that very Spirit intercedes with sighs too deep for words. And God, who searches the heart, knows what is the mind of the Spirit, because the Spirit intercedes for the saints according to the will of God. (Rom. 8:26-27)

The Holy Spirit is God present in you and for you, to do today what God has always done—bring the kingdom of God to the lives of God's people. God through the Spirit will do for you what you cannot do for yourself. You may not know how or for what to pray in many situations in life. The discernment of God's will and purpose may be difficult in a given situation, but God through the Spirit will pray the prayer that needs to be prayed.

This passage gives you another glimpse of grace at work, this time in the arena of prayer. God will do the work of prayer for you as you offer up your dilemma, problem, or concern and surrender control of the solution. God's grace is set to work in the mystery that is the Trinity. The divine community of the Creator, Son, and Holy Spirit speak, listen, and respond to each other within the circle of your concern. God is at work in you, for you, and through you that God's will might be done. As in faith and humility you offer up your weakness, however it may express itself in your life, the Spirit will be at work interceding for you according to the will of God.

This deep experience of prayer takes place within your very center. You will encounter these prayer opportunities whenever you face those moments of profound grief, despair, pain, or addiction. Surrender them to the Spirit within so that the prayers that need to be prayed will be prayed.

The Holy Spirit is involved in another but similar type of prayer. Many Christians experience praying in the Spirit, or praying in tongues, as it is sometimes called. Praying in tongues is a non-rational experience of prayer. The pray-er does not consciously control what is being said. In fact, the pray-er is not using a language he or she knows. This prayer, prayed by the Spirit through the person who has surrendered conscious control, edifies the spirit of the person praying. That is, it upbuilds and strengthens the spiritual dimension of the person—relationship with God, joy in God's presence, and sensitivity to spiritual understanding.

Praying in the Spirit is a manifestation of the Spirit's presence and is one of many spiritual gifts given by God through the Spirit for the ministry and mission of the church.

You can request this gift from God through prayer. Pray also for wisdom, humility, and, most of all, love. All spiritual gifts are dangerous if directed by a proud and possessive ego. Praying in the Spirit, as well as other spiritual gifts, is meant to be a blessing to you and others under the direction of God's love.

Read the following Bible passages to explore more fully how the Bible describes this form of prayer and its use: 1 Corinthians 14; Acts 19:1-7.

As you might expect, all three persons of the Trinity are involved in your prayer life as they are involved in your faith relationship to God. Each person of the Trinity may be addressed in prayer. Each person of the Trinity is involved in the response to your prayer. There is no end to the excitement and adventure this kind of relationship holds for you, especially for your prayer life.

Prayer and Language

When we pray to God, to whom are we praying? What are the images that suggest the language of prayer? What experiences and information have formed the images that dictate what words we use in prayer?

These questions are important because they form the background for the way we pray.

The images of God and the language of prayer may come from several sources. One is the experience we have in the worship setting. Styles of prayer in public worship often convey the way people think they ought to pray. Another source may be the prayer experiences of childhood—listening to the prayers of a parent at mealtime or bedtime.

The Bible provides, for most people, the images and often the language of prayer. Whole generations can be nurtured on a particular Bible translation that will shape their understanding of God and the language that should be used in prayer.

This is true of the original King James Version. For years it was the primary translation used in the English-speaking world. God was addressed as "Thee" and "Thou." In more recent times, as translations have changed the language in which God is addressed in the Bible, many people find themselves addressing God as "you." One speaks to God in the same way one may speak to a neighbor or friend, using the common language spoken between humans.

Using a distinct language for God—"thee" and "thou," for instance—stresses the otherness of God—God's transcendence. It conveys the sense that communication with God is different from communication with another human. Using such language may also denote an understanding of a special relationship with God that is different from any other relationship a person has.

On the other hand, to use the same language for prayer as that used in every other relationship stresses closeness and familiarity

21

with God. It emphasizes the immanence of God, the presence of God within and among us. The same language is used for God that is used in communicating with others.

Jesus, on occasion, used the word, "Abba" for God in prayer. This is an Aramaic word that most Bible translators interpret as "Father." However, in English the word carries much more the sense of "Daddy" or "Papa." This is obviously a very informal and intimate term for God.

Another source of imagery for understanding God comes from our experience. Personal spiritual experiences of God may provide images that will influence how one thinks of God and addresses God. People who have shared these experiences report that some of them have created a deep sense of awe and otherness of God, while others have discovered an intimate nearness and informality in God's presence.

Whether you use a formal or informal language to address God is a question you will want to ask yourself. How do you understand and image the God to whom you pray? What language best expresses that for you—formal or informal, common or special?

Another concern in the area of prayer and language is the role of feminine and masculine metaphors for God in shaping our images and prayer language.

With the rise of feminine consciousness, our traditions have been revisited in the light of this new awareness. The predominant images of God in our Western culture and church have been masculine. These images that contain what we traditionally have named masculine characteristics have shaped much of the thinking and praying of the church. Traditionally the pronoun "he" has been used almost exclusively with reference to God. The use of such language and images has tended to create the idea that God is totally male.

However, the Bible teaches that God is spirit, neither male nor female. Yet for us to speak of God or to God, we have to use the language derived from images related to our experience and learning. Language is derived from our experiences of being masculine or feminine. When we speak of someone we image a person having certain characteristics and qualities that fall into these two categories. The same is true of God. The Scriptures contain metaphors for God that are labeled masculine or feminine, that is, they tend

22

to be identified with men or women. We do not have any other way of understanding it.

Because our tradition is patriarchal the masculine God as Father has dominated in image and language for God. "Mother" is not a name most Christians would apply to God, even though the Bible contains many mothering metaphors.

Many women and men today are seeking to make the language of worship and prayer more inclusive of feminine images and language. It is a difficult struggle. Women have been relegated to a lesser role, and religious leadership has been predominately male. However, as we reform our awareness and exposure to feminine images of God and begin to see the fullness of God expressed in all sorts of activity that cover the full range of human need, we will be able to reimage God and find ourselves free to use inclusive language.

There is a name God used in the Bible that is not related to a specific activity and, therefore, appears to be free from gender identification. When Moses was confronted by God through the burning bush Moses asked God's name. God replied with the name "I Am"—a name that is all-inclusive of being and of time and the very ground of being. The activity of God, I Am, in the lives of people and in creation can be imaged by all of the ways in which we act as men and women. God has been imaged in the Bible as warrior, judge, father (Deut. 1:31), comforting mother (Isa. 66:13), plus many others. It is important to remember that these are metaphors for God that describe relationships of inter-action and not the essence or nature of God.

It is interesting to note that in two prominent places where the personification of God is described, the metaphors are feminine. One is the Shekinah, a term used to describe that mysterious visible presence of God among the people of Israel, and the other is Wisdom or Sophia (Prov. 8).

In the New Testament, too, Jesus tells two parables in Luke 15 that use both masculine and feminine metaphors for God. They are the parables of the shepherd who leaves the ninety-nine sheep to find the one separated from the flock, and the woman who had ten coins but lost one of them and searched diligently until she found it. The same truth is being expressed in two different stories. The difference is that in the one, God is pictured as a shepherd, and in the other, God is pictured as a woman in search of her lost coin.

If you were to compose prayers based on these two parables and their message of God reaching out to the lost, they could read something like this:

> O God, Shepherd of the world, I thank you for diligently risking all to find me and carry me back to the fold of your people. Amen.

> O God, Woman of patient compassion, I thank you for being willing to look in the dark corners of the world to save your lost ones. I thank you for your diligent search for me when I hide beneath the dust under the bed. Amen.

The issue is not that we have to choose between using masculine or feminine images and language for God, but that both are to be embraced so that the fullness of God's revelation can be experienced. Out of that experience we can begin to reimage God and gain courage to express in the language of our prayers a full awareness of the wonder and mystery of God.

At the same time, it will give to women and men the knowledge and experience that they are created equally in the image of God, inasmuch as God is willing to be among us in masculine or feminine activity.

For men, allowing the feminine metaphors equal footing with the masculine may create tension and discomfort. But growth usually involves such discomfort. Explore this area of prayer so that your devotional life can be enriched by a broader awareness of God's activity. You will probably discover parts of yourself that will respond more positively to prayer as the feminine within you is acknowledged and allowed expression. This can be a liberating experience as you find wholeness as a man.

For women, this exploration in broadening the images and language of prayer can be a liberating experience as well. Because masculine metaphors have dominated so much of religious expression, discovering the feminine in images and language for prayer will affirm who you are and free you from relying only on masculine metaphors in your devotional expression. This may be particularly helpful if you have been victimized or felt put down as a woman within the religious community, your family, or the community at large.

To find your language and voice in prayer is important. Let your prayer be yours. You have a relationship with God and God desires to hear what you think, feel, experience, and desire. As you read the Bible and reflect on the God you have experienced in Jesus Christ and your community of faith, let the images create a language that for you will release gratitude, praise, concern, and compassion.

Prayer and the Body

When you pray, your body is not just hanging out, waiting for the rest of you to be finished. Your body-self is a part of your prayer experience and expression. You are a whole person, and all of you participates in what you are doing. If you ignore parts of yourself you hinder the full experience of this activity.

What does the body have to do with prayer? I was a student intern from seminary serving a church in North Dakota. It was Lent and I was presiding at my first communion service at this church. When it came time in the service for the prayer of confession, I turned to the altar, knelt, and began to pray the long confessional prayer. When the prayer was done I stood up and turned to announce the words of forgiveness. I was shocked. Everybody had left the church! My eyes quickly surveyed the whole sanctuary and everyone was gone. Some seconds went by as I stood there in shocked silence. Then I noticed the top of one head slowly rising to eye level from behind a pew. Suddenly I knew what had happened. Everyone, from the youngest to the oldest, was kneeling on the floor with their folded hands and heads resting on the seats of the pew. I spoke the words of forgiveness, they stood, and the service went on. I had never seen this before, but this was a long-standing tradition in this congregation. Confessing was an act of the body as well as the mind, will, and emotions.

All religions use some particular forms of body posture in prayer. In fact, in some it is required. Five times a day a devout Muslim will kneel and face Mecca to pray. Yoga as a prayer discipline focuses on body positions. Folded hands, bent heads, kneeling, standing, and sitting are all body actions related to prayer.

25

Some Christians kneel to pray. Others stand. Still others sit. Different types of prayer may call for different postures.

Something different may be experienced through your body that does not come through your mind or feelings. A deeper sense of humility may be expressed through kneeling. An experience of total commitment or adoration may be felt by lying prostrate on the floor. Standing may give a sense of being uplifted. Sitting will provide a more comfortable, focused position for a long period of prayer.

If you have not experienced various postures in praying, you may want to explore these and see if they are a help in a more complete prayer expression.

In the Letter to the Romans the apostle Paul urges Christians to respond totally to God's grace and mercy by giving their whole selves in worship and service:

> I appeal to you therefore, brothers and sisters, by the mercies of God, to present your bodies as a living sacrifice, holy and acceptable to God which is your spiritual worship. (Rom. 12:1)

If you are praying without conscious consideration of your body, you are leaving out an important component of your prayer experience.

When you were a child, you were probably taught to fold your hands when you prayed, to keep from being distracted by playing with things around you. Prayer is a focused activity and being distracted by thinking or doing things not connected with prayer hinders your concentration.

Especially in Asia the hands placed together and held in front of the body is a sign of respect and honor, and is used by Asians and others in prayer. Some people raise their hands as a sign for blessing God with praise. This was a practice among the Old Testament pray-ers, as seen in Psalm 134:2: "Lift up your hands to the holy place, and bless the Lord."

Again you may want to experiment and discover which ways of expressing prayer with your hands add to your experience of prayer.

Praying with hands open to God is a symbol that can have a powerful effect on the attitude of prayer. Often we approach God with our hands clenched tightly around our needs, fears, or possessions. We come to talk with God but continue to try to keep some things hidden. To show hands open and empty reveals to God that we have given up our attachments. We extend our open hands, ready to receive what God will give. In his book *With Open Hands*, Henri J. M. Nouwen notes: "The resistance to praying is like the resistance of tightly clenched fists. This image shows the tension, the desire to cling tightly to yourself, a greediness which betrays fear."[1]

Sometimes the body can lead the heart to a place of openness and receptivity towards God. Lifting open hands extended out toward God, you may find your heart more willing to surrender to God. Kneeling may, as well, encourage your spirit to bend in honest humility. Making the body still, eyes closed, embracing silence, your soul may see itself in a new way.

In many cultures dance is part of the prayer experience. In dance the body is allowed to give full expression to what the prayer feels toward God and desires to receive from God.

When God liberated the people of Israel from Egypt and led them safely across the Red Sea, their response was singing and dancing to express their joy and thanksgiving:

> Then the prophet Miriam, Aaron's sister, took a tambourine in her hand; and all the women went out after her with tambourines and with dancing. And Miriam sang to them: "Sing to the Lord, for he has triumphed gloriously; horse and rider he has thrown into the sea." (Exod. 15:20-21)

In mainline Christian denominations in Europe and the United States, dance became separated from religious worship. Dance was categorized as secular activity. Emotions and ecstasy in the church were something to be avoided. It became important to sit still, kneel still, and stand still. In many churches excessive movement is suspect. However, a renewal of liturgical dance is bringing this form of prayer back into the church.

You may want to experiment by using dance in your personal prayer. Play a tape of liturgical music such as a song of praise, a form of the Kyrie, or a hymn that will express what you want to offer up in prayer. As you play the music, let your body respond with movement that expresses what you are feeling—joy, thankfulness, compassion for others, pain, or a desire for forgiveness. Offer it up to God with your heart, soul, mind, and body.

There are other ways in which you can relate to prayer with your body. Some people find that their prayer response to God is enhanced when they are in nature walking, or running laps, or engaged in some activity where the body is actively involved and their senses are being used to relate to the world around them.

As you explore various forms of prayer, you will discover those that are best for you. Do not hesitate to experiment with several types of prayer.

Some find it helpful to have a special or designated place for prayer where they live. This may be a particular chair or room in the house. A prayer center could be created to provide a focus for prayer with a table on which candles, a cross, or an icon is placed. Articles from nature such as flowers, rocks, or a tree branch could be included. Some find a designated place helpful to maintain a discipline of prayer and provide a stimulus for their prayer and meditation.

Again, experiment to see if these are ways that can enrich your prayer life.

Facing Obstacles to Prayer

Prayer is not without its struggles. Prayer can become difficult because of lack of knowledge, or your own inner attitudes, or the failure to follow specific principles of spiritual discipline. In your prayer journey you will probably encounter most of these obstacles. Even those who are considered giants in the disciplines of prayer and spirituality share how they have encountered these struggles. No one is immune from these questions and problems.

WHY DON'T I PRAY?

This question may be a shortened version of a whole host of similar questions. "Why don't I pray like Mr. Smith or Mrs. Jones? Why don't I pray except in crises? Why don't I feel like praying as much as I should?"

Such questions suggest that the problem could involve several issues. One of these is the struggle that the church calls the enemies of spiritual life—the devil, the world, and our own flesh. Just as prayer is centered in a relationship with a personal God, so overcoming the inertia to pray involves struggling with the enemies of that relationship. The tendency to live without God is always present. This tendency can be fed by guilt. If you have not been praying as you feel you should, you may think that God is angry, so you are afraid to come to God. Such guilt and fear can easily quench the desire to pray. Recalling God's forgiving grace and responding to the image of Jesus standing at the door gently knocking may encourage you to pray.

The experience of grace nurtures the desire to pray. This is why the daily practice of confession and forgiveness is so important. It will keep you centered in God's love and provide an environment for the Holy Spirit to stir your desire to pray in response to this experience of love. Think about the experience many farm families had with their hand pump. Until they primed it with water they could not draw water from the pump. Prayer will not flow easily from your life without the priming action of the Holy Spirit flooding you with grace.

In addition to your own tendency to go about life without God, there is the presence of those forces of evil that are against the purposes of God in the world and your life. They would like nothing better than to have you not pray. Ask God to deliver and protect you from the spirit of the age of the unbelieving world and the evil one. A strong note of warning and encouragement is found in 1 Peter 5:8:

> Discipline yourselves, keep alert. Like a roaring lion your adversary the devil prowls around, looking for someone to devour.

Another way to find help to overcome apathy is by praying with others. It may help to find a prayer partner, one with whom you meet regularly to share prayer time and discussion. This may be a formal situation in which someone may serve as your spiritual director, or at other times it may be a friend with whom you share this prayer time. Your prayer companion and you will encourage and strengthen each other.

THE WAY I PRAY DOESN'T FEEL RIGHT.

This obstacle may arise when you have learned to pray in a way that does not fit who you are. Most of us have learned to pray from others who have shared their particular way of praying. You may find that it just does not seem to fit with your own person. This is understandable because we are different. Temperaments vary and personal preferences for the way things are perceived and expressed will differ from person to person.

In recent years considerable study in prayer and temperament types has been carried out. Based on personal preferences for perceiving or judging information, being centered in thinking or feeling functions, or preferring to get information from your senses or intuition, you will find some styles of prayer more natural for you. These differences, as well as other individual traits, suggest that you might experiment with various prayer forms. Books related to this subject are noted in the Further Reading section.

It is important to find your own way in this so that prayer will be a natural and honest expression of who you are. Then you will feel free to focus on the particular prayer ministry to which God is calling you.

I DON'T KNOW HOW TO PRAY ON MY OWN.

As a child you were dependent on others to teach you how to pray. You learned to memorize prayers given to you by adults. You identified with the way your parents, Sunday school teachers, and pastors modeled prayer. This is the way it was for most of us. This is true not only for prayer but for most of the other activities of the religious life.

The expectation is that each of us would come into ownership of the ways we would relate to God. However, many adults do not develop their own moral and spiritual understanding and practice and remain dependent on others.

Take up the challenge to move beyond dependency on others and only on external religious practices as the expression of your relationship to God. You are called to take the steps to own your faith and prayer life. This involves developing inner spirituality and authority, taking responsibility for trust, sharing yourself with God in prayer, and making your own commitments.

Some people have given up on Christianity and the church because it seemed oppressive or failed them in a crisis. They became adults in terms of responsibilities and problems but failed at the same time to move toward an adult faith and spiritual discipline. It is no wonder that their spirituality became inadequate.

This does not mean that the church or Christian parents have not failed some people. They have. If this is your situation, the point is not to fix blame but to direct you to move on in developing a mature faith. Childhood faith and experience are important and appropriate. When you become an adult, however, the childlike trust should remain, but the personal, adult ownership of prayer should also be present.

The important thing is to begin praying. Share your thoughts, concerns, and requests with God. Speak to God as you would to any other person. You may find it helpful to begin by speaking your prayers rather than silently thinking them.

WHY DON'T I FEEL ANYTHING?

You will discover dry times in your prayer life. In the rhythm of the spiritual life the desert has its place. Prayer may feel as if nothing is happening. The important thing is not to give up in those times. The good feelings of prayer will return. Be careful at this point not to succumb to the thought that prayer has to be felt to be effective or meaningful. Primarily you pray out of a foundation of faith and obedience. Secondarily you pray out of emotion. After a few experiences of praying through the dry times, you begin to realize that the vibrant and creative times will return.

It is not unusual for prayer to have a rhythm, as do so many aspects of life. Those times when you feel flat and totally unexcited about prayer may be a period of incubation. Also it may be a time for internal adjustments in your inner life. Then again it may be the prelude to an exciting leap of awareness or new spiritual consciousness. All of these experiences have been a part of what I have encountered in times like these.

It has also been my experience that new Christians or newly awakened Christians are blessed by God with quick and direct answers to prayer, as if God is encouraging them in their new-found or renewed faith.

A young man from India expressed an interest in exploring Christianity. He had become disillusioned with Hinduism. I encouraged him to read the Bible and several other books about Christianity. He attended worship regularly. We met on a regular basis to discuss his reading and progress. He was attracted to Jesus and Christianity but found himself unable to make a commitment. He would not stand and say the creed in the worship service. This went on for a few months. Then, early one Monday morning he came to see me. He told me that during the service he found himself standing with the congregation reciting the Apostles' Creed. It was as if God had pulled him to his feet and the Holy Spirit had generated a commitment in faith to everything he was saying.

During the next few weeks, he went through a series of crises that included losing his job. In each crisis he would come to the church and ask me to pray with him. God swiftly answered each of his needs during that time.

As time went on, he continued to believe as fervently but found that his prayers were not always answered so immediately. He began to learn some of the deeper lessons of discipleship—patient waiting on the Lord, praying to deepen the relationship and not just to ask for things, staying disciplined in prayer, worship, and Scripture reading even though it was not always exciting.

WHY DON'T I GET AN ANSWER?

The question of unanswered prayer often comes up. It is possible to speculate about the answer to this question, but in the end it may not be possible to provide a neat solution to this dilemma. God invites and encourages us to pray. God promises to hear and answer our prayers. However, that for which we pray does not always happen.

Several things could enter into the dynamics of prayer and give some clues as to why answers do not seem to appear for some of our prayers.

Timing is one important aspect. Prayers may not be answered immediately. We may be expecting an immediate answer, but in the long run circumstances may not be ready for the answer to be beneficial. All things may not be in place. Many times our prayers are answered through the agency of other people and within the process of what is happening around us. Working out of a natural process takes time to unfold. The best answer to your prayer may take time to arrange. God has always worked through history and the processes of nature and community. Even in the sending of Jesus, the apostle Paul reminds us that he was sent in the "fullness of time," that is, when everything was ready (Gal. 4:4).

The poet Rainer Maria von Rilke reminds us that you often have to live with the question until you are ready to live with the answer. The same may be true of your prayer. Are you ready to live with what you ask for? God's delay in answering may be allowing for preparation time to live with the answer.

What God may have in store for you is different from what you asked. It may be better or just different. Often it is a surprise. Keep your eyes open to what is happening and realize that the answer may be there in a different form.

I was visiting a church camp, and while there a man with whom I was talking asked that I pray for him. He had been feeling very anxious and unable to sleep. He wanted me to pray that God would heal this condition and give him back his serenity and sense of peace. I began to pray with him but sensed that I did not have the whole story. I asked him about recent events in his life. He told me that God had blessed him in a wonderful way through a large sum of money. The government had made a mistake in a payment to him and sent several thousand dollars too much. He looked upon this as a blessing from God and did not report the mistake. He was intending to use that money. He seemed overjoyed at this windfall. In his own mind he did not see any conflict that could be causing his anxiety and sleeplessness. I now felt ready to pray with him, but my prayer was much different from the one he was expecting. His eyes were opened to the moral conflict he was feeling in his unconscious mind. He promised to pay back the money. And if he did, I am sure his anxiety left and sleep returned.

I am surprised at how our conscious mind will not see the truth in front of us. It is easy to become blind to what is really happening and focus our prayers on the wrong thing. This man's request for prayer became an opportunity for his prayer to be answered in truth and integrity. God's answer was a surprise. And with the help of some Christian friends, he was able to face and live with that answer.

Waiting on the Lord is another key virtue of the Christian. Patience is one of the expressions of the fruit of the Spirit (Gal. 5:22). Having prayed, perhaps continuously, you are not to give up too soon. If the desire of the prayer is still with you, continue to pray. None really knows how long God will take to answer any prayer.

The prophet Isaiah brought this word of the Lord to the people of Israel in exile:

> Why do you say, O Jacob, and speak, O Israel,
> "My way is hidden from the Lord,
>   and my right is disregarded by my God"?
> Have you not known? Have you not heard?
> The Lord is the everlasting God,
>   the Creator of the ends of the earth.
> He does not faint or grow weary;
>   his understanding is unsearchable.
> He gives power to the faint, and strengthens the powerless.
> Those who wait for the Lord shall renew their strength,
>   they shall mount up with wings like eagles. (Isa. 40:27-29, 31a)

For seventy years the people of Israel prayed for an end to the exile. Finally, it came.

I believe God answers all prayer. The answers may be different from what I expect. Any number of reasons could lie behind the answer that appears.

You may not be praying in accordance with God's will. Ask to be guided in your prayer. Your first prayer can be the request for the prayer you are to pray.

Keep focused on your relationship with God and affirm that God is for you and will be working on your behalf, even if the outcome is not as you want. Learn to live with the truth expressed by the apostle Paul in Romans 8:28, "We know that all things work together for good for those who love God, who are called according to his purpose." You cannot see around the corner and do not know the future. But you can trust that God will be at work in every situation to redeem and transform it.

34

There are no guarantees that your life will be spared difficulty, hardship, tragedy, or disease. We cannot control everything around us. Not even does God choose to control everything that happens in the world, though he may intervene at times. However, God can redeem every situation. Through God's people, operating with God's compassion, gifts of grace through the Spirit and good will, God wants to transform every community, family, nation, and person.

In the meantime, offer your needs to God and trust God's steadfast love and promise to hear and answer your prayer, knowing that you are not abandoned in this world.

ARE YOU EXPECTING ENOUGH FROM GOD?

What are the limits of prayer? How far dare we go in making requests of God? Do our expectations influence prayer? These questions probe an area of prayer over which there is much discussion and not a little controversy. That is usually the situation when we explore the fine line between God's ultimate control over answers to prayer and our capacity to influence God by our prayers. Facing such paradoxes can either leave us with a sense of futility or motivate us to explore and test the limits.

There are numerous biblical references that encourage us to lift our expectations. They imply that we usually aim too low, either in our motivation or our expectation. The Epistle of James warns us to consider prayer as an option for getting what we want, rather than acting out of greed, covetousness, or deceit. The writer is saying that we should look to God for what we need and not use the methods of the world.

> You do not have, because you do not ask. You ask and do not receive, because you ask wrongly, in order to spend what you get on your pleasures. (James 4:2-3)

In the Letter to the Ephesians the apostle Paul describes the capacity of God to give far more than we can ask or imagine. In this benediction he offers us an image to inspire expectant prayer:

> Now to him who by the power at work within us is able to accomplish abundantly far more than all we can ask or imagine, to him be glory in the church and in Christ Jesus to all generations, forever and ever. Amen. (Eph. 3:20-21)

In the Sermon on the Mount Jesus teaches that God personally knows our needs. He warns against letting our prayer become merely a prideful demonstration for others or a heaping up of many words, as if quantity would make the difference. He also discourages anxious striving for the things we need. Rather, seek after the kingdom of God and God's righteousness and these things will come to us. Notice in these verses from the Sermon on the Mount the simple way Jesus encourages us to pray with high expectation:

> But whenever you pray, go into your room and shut the door and pray to your Father who is in secret; and your Father who sees in secret will reward you. (Matt. 6:6)

> Your Father knows what you need before you ask him. (Matt. 6:8)

Jesus encourages us to be bold in prayer and to have high expectations in our asking: "Whatever you ask for in prayer with faith, you will receive" (Matt. 21:22).

Praying in accordance with God's will and rooted in faith, we are encouraged to ask for whatever we will. God is ready and willing to be the loving Parent blessing the child who comes in trust and obedience.

DO YOU REMEMBER TO SAY THANK YOU?

When you read the story of Jesus healing ten lepers, the ending comes as something of a shock. They were cured on their way to show themselves to the priest. However, only one returns to Jesus when he sees that he is made well. Jesus' question when this man returns is the question we would all ask: "Where are the other nine?"

It is hard to imagine experiencing that kind of healing and failing to return to give thanks. Yet that is not so unusual. We seem to have a difficult time remembering the giver of our blessings.

When you pray and receive an answer, the prayer is not complete until you have given thanks. In the act of gratitude the blessing becomes more complete. You have completed the circle by acknowledging the One from whom the answer has come.

Jesus' response to the one leper who returned to give thanks is to declare that he has not only been cured but made whole. His healing had become part of his relationship with Jesus, and by returning and giving thanks he had been brought into a deeper relationship with him.

I have seen this experience repeated in people who come to our church's Sunday evening healing service. On occasion, individuals who have experienced healing will come back to offer prayers of thanksgiving to God for their healing. In that act I sense a deeper healing taking place within them—a strengthening of their relationship with God and a great joy in God's activity in their lives.

Giving thanks is the best antidote to bitterness and cynicism. It is hard to give thanks and still maintain a mean or bitter spirit.

Each day find ways to give thanks in prayer so that it becomes a natural way to act. Pray at meal times. At the end of the day remember all of the ways in which God has blessed you. Recall the specific prayers God has answered for you, and offer thanks for them.

Gratitude for answered prayer nurtures the spirit of prayer in your life. If you continually acknowledge God as the giver of all good gifts in your life and the One who answers prayer, you will live with a much greater awareness of God's presence and grace in your life.

Praying with Others

Prayer is communal as well as personal. Religious expression is a shared experience among all people. This can occur in formalized liturgy, spontaneous prayer in small groups, or family rituals.

Spiritual intimacy in groups is experienced in prayer. People who share in prayer band together at a deep level and experience a fellowship of the spirit that unites them around the center of their faith. For Christians this experience is an expression of being the Body of Christ, the church. In this shared prayer there is a common experience of the presence of the Holy Spirit that makes manifest the reality of the church. People are linked together in this experience and come to know and care for each other. A spiritual community is born out of this shared prayer and love.

PRAYING THE LITURGY

Liturgy refers to the worship pattern a group of Christians use to worship together. Some churches use an historic liturgy, others a new form or spontaneous creation.

The public prayer life of a congregation fulfills many purposes. These include building up the sense of community through common prayer; witnessing to the larger community of its life of faith, love, and hope; providing encouragement to live rightly; receiving God's gifts of grace with gratitude and joy; maintaining a connectedness with others so that you may pray and support them; receiving the prayers and support of others.

In the liturgy you celebrate a common life with other Christians. Certain parts of the liturgy are meant to be a common prayer. In these prayers your own particular life becomes joined to the others present, and each life is a piece of one voice in prayer. The confession of sins, the Kyrie, hymn of praise, intercessory prayer, prayer of the day, and other common prayers bring the community together.

As you pray these common prayers, your thoughts can reflect the particular aspects of your own life, the needs of those of whom you are aware, and the particular issues that concern you.

Common liturgical prayer does not mean that you don't have to think, feel, or contribute. It is not a time to put yourself on hold and merely observe someone else praying for you. It is a time to link your own unique life with the lives of others. You actively participate by bringing your praise, your thanks, your time, your concerns, your needs.

There are certain times in the liturgy when you can exercise personal prayer. The prelude is a time for quiet, reflective prayer in which you prepare to bring your life into the liturgy and prepare yourself to receive the word, sacrament, and blessing of God.

At the time of the Communion distribution you can pray for the others who are taking Communion with you. Pray for their needs and for God's blessing. This will enhance your sense of community with them and exercise the love you receive from God toward others.

PRAYING IN THE FAMILY

Family rituals and prayer times are another experience of corporate prayer.

There are the usual times when families often pray—meal times, bed time, and upon rising in the morning. In addition, family corporate prayers can be shared before taking a trip, returning home, anniversaries, birthdays, and times of special needs or crises.

Initiating and sustaining a family prayer life will deepen the intimacy of the family and help develop the spiritual life of everyone involved. Children will grow up realizing that it is natural to relate all of life to God.

Because of the different personalities of members of the family, it is important to vary the form of praying so that all can relate to it. Use items like candles, crosses, and pictures. Prayer reminders like Advent wreaths or Lenten activities will help those who are more sensate to relate to prayer. Shared silence, music, and praying specifically for individual members of the family will offer variety.

As children grow older allow them to develop in their prayer experience. They can share in leadership in the devotional time and create family rituals.

Explore family devotional aids at your Christian bookstore. It is just as important to shop diligently for spiritual food for your family as it is to shop for physical food at the grocery store.

Let your creativity nurture your family prayer time so that it remains vital, exciting, and real. Keep your family prayer life related to the daily events in the lives of family members.

One of the greatest benefits your family will experience as you pray is the way in which each one will feel blessed by God. It is an asset to live each day with the knowledge that God is blessing your life.

In the Old Testament God gave a prayer blessing for the people of Israel. Many churches use it in their services. It could be used in your home each day:

The Lord bless you and keep you;
the Lord make his face to shine upon you, and be gracious
    to you;
the Lord lift up his countenance upon you, and give you
    peace. (Num. 6:24-26)

You can find other prayer blessings in Scripture that you can use in your family prayer time: Romans 15:13; 2 Corinthians

13:13; 1 Thessalonians 5:23; 2 Thessalonians 3:16; Hebrews 13:20-21.

One of the wonderful privileges our Lord has given us in prayer is the power to bless others in God's name. Use that privilege often in your family. They will be blessed.

PRAYING IN SMALL GROUPS

A vital component to Christian spirituality is the practice of meeting and praying in small groups. It provides an experience of developing the ability to pray spontaneously and conversationally. As you learn to know the others in a small group setting, you can more freely share your needs and respond in prayer to the needs of others. The small group provides an intimacy and sense of fellowship that cannot be achieved with large groups or in a formal liturgy.

Jesus took Peter, James, and John with him for prayer in intense and deep moments. On the Mount of Transfiguration and in the Garden of Gethsemane, Jesus desired a small group to share with him in his ecstasy and his agony. Jesus also emphasized the role of small groups in experiencing his presence. "For where two or three are gathered in my name, I am there among them" (Matt. 18:20).

There is a supportive strength in the presence of other Christians with whom you share a deep prayer fellowship. Jesus sent his disciples out two by two rather than alone. The apostle Paul traveled with Christian companions on his missionary journeys.

Small groups will develop your capacity both to minister to the needs of others and to be ministered to. It will enable you to see your prayer ministry touch the lives of others with care and healing.

Seek out people with whom you are comfortable and compatible—persons who have the same spirit of prayer that you have. They do not need to be just like you; they just need to be drawn by the same desire to pray and grow in the fellowship of Christ's presence.

A prayer group can be three to five persons. Leadership should be shared and the focus on prayer maintained. When your group grows larger, form new groups so that the size of the group remains small.

Many people attribute significant spiritual growth to their experience in a small prayer group. You will find that it adds a dynamic dimension to your prayer life.

2

Prayer as Request

The first steps in prayer are often taken as a cry of desperation. Things have gotten out of hand. The world is pressing in. A terrible disaster hits. Sickness comes. Life makes no sense.

You come to God, asking for a change for the better. Rescue me. Meet my needs. Heal me. Change my partner. Forgive my sins. Give me courage. Help me pass this test. Is such prayer appropriate?

If your life is yours alone to figure out and handle, then such prayer might not be appropriate, but your life is not yours alone. You have not been created by God and then abandoned to live out life by yourself. God has clearly demonstrated a desire to be a part of your life.

When our first parents in the Garden of Eden broke the relationship with God and began to suffer the consequences of their rebellion, God appeared and held out to them a promise to be at work to save them.

When the descendants of Abraham found themselves in bondage in Egypt, destined to live as slaves with no freedom or hope for themselves, God's saving action appeared. God heard the cries of his people and raised up for them the leader Moses. Throughout the story of humankind is woven the story of God's gracious action on behalf of people everywhere. God is interested in his people and invites them to look to God for help.

In various ways Jesus also describes for us a way to understand how God seeks to come to our aid in the human situations that almost overcome our lives.

In the Gospel of Luke Jesus shares a story that illustrates the heart of God for his children:

> Is there anyone among you who, if your child asks for a fish, will give a snake instead of a fish? Or if the child asks for an egg, will give a scorpion? If you then, who are evil, know how to give good gifts to your children, how much more will the heavenly Father give the Holy Spirit to those who ask him! (Luke 11:11-13)

Throughout his ministry, Jesus presented God as a loving Parent who draws his children close to him. Particularly close to Jesus' heart and concern were the outcast and abandoned. He was there for the sick, demon-possessed, sinners, children, women, and others who were pushed to the margins of society. The beginning experience of Jesus for most people is the experience of Jesus as Savior. That is, they meet him at the points of their need and his gracious response. God has taken the initiative to enter into the human situation and to be the Savior of those who have a need for help from beyond, and that is all of us.

God is not some impersonal force quite separate and distant from you. God is not some unknown wish concocted by a human brain to fill in the gaps of human ignorance. The experience of the people of God is that God is personal and interacts to save and give life to them.

This is the God to whom we pray—a Savior, a Shepherd, a loving Parent, a Healer, a caring One. This God is known by the way in which his word is primarily a saving act through the person of Jesus of Nazareth. And this action calls out to us to draw near and ask. The most simple and direct words about prayer that Jesus uttered are:

> Ask, and it will be given you; search, and you will find; knock, and the door will be opened for you. For everyone who asks receives, and everyone who searches finds, and for everyone who knocks, the door will be opened. (Luke 11:9-10)

These words are a clear invitation to allow God to be a part of whatever we need.

There are countless stories from the Bible and other human experiences that demonstrate this saving action of God in response to prayer. One of these stories is the dramatic testimony of Gert Behanna, which I heard her share.

Gert was a woman reared in the lap of luxury. However, her life was marked by extreme spiritual poverty. She really had no desire for or consciousness of God in her life. She was married several times. Her life became dominated by her addiction to alcohol. One day, in a deep despair over her life, she thought about suicide. There seemed to be no future for her and little hope for change.

In her despair she cried out to God, or whoever might be out there beyond herself to help her. She found herself immediately calm and felt a strong sense of another presence with her. An inner voice seemed to be directing her to seek out someone to talk to. She went to a little church down the street and talked to the pastor. As he talked with her and prayed with her, faith was born within her. The journey was not easy, but her life changed. God was there for her, as God has been there for thousands who have called out.

Your needs and their solutions may not be as dramatic as Gert Behanna's. But the lesson is still the same. God is there waiting for the knock on the door. Whoever knocks will find God desiring to open the door to his gracious saving acts.

Prayer and God's Providence

One of the questions that emerges in discussions about prayer is, Why pray if God already knows what is going to happen? Doesn't this predetermine what will take place? This difficult question is not easily solved in a logical way. It is another of those areas of our relationship with God where we are thrown into a paradox.

On the one hand, it is true that God is all knowing and God's purpose will be done. On the other hand, we are commanded and encouraged to pray with all confidence that our prayers make a difference.

When we face such paradoxes, it is best to act with what we know rather than with what we do not know. In fact, it is better to act than to become paralyzed by the paradox.

You could spend a lifetime puzzling over this dilemma and trying to arrive at a logical, rational solution and never enter into the act of prayer itself. Or you could let yourself become a total cynic and say that prayer is not real because you cannot understand it or prove it by some scientific method.

Historically some philosophers and even some cultures have succumbed to thinking of the future as totally fixed and in place. They have tried to express this by devising a philosophy of fate—what will be, will be. Total acceptance of the current situation is accepted, and no attempt is made to change.

In the biblical tradition, however, we find a call to change. Judgments are withheld when repentance is expressed. Healing occurs when life is offered to God. Minds are changed when confronted by God's truth. The act of prayer is found in all of these situations.

King Hezekiah of Israel became very sick and was at the point of death. The prophet Isaiah came to him and said, "Set your house in order, for you shall die; you shall not recover." The story goes on in this way:

> Then Hezekiah turned his face to the wall, and prayed to the Lord: "Remember now, O Lord, I implore you, how I have walked before you in faithfulness with a whole heart, and have done what is good in your sight." And Hezekiah wept bitterly.
>
> Then the word of the Lord came to Isaiah: "Go and say to Hezekiah, Thus says the Lord, the God of your ancestor David: I have heard your prayer, I have seen your tears; I will add fifteen years to your life." (Isa. 38:1-5)

In the Book of Genesis you can read the story of Abraham pleading for the cities of Sodom and Gomorrah. Each time he prays, God consents to withhold judgment if enough righteous people are found. However, in the end there are not enough and the cities are destroyed, but God was willing to change the judgment (Gen. 18:20-33).

In the New Testament, Jesus teaches about persistence in prayer. In Luke's Gospel we read this parable and teaching:

> Then Jesus told them a parable about their need to pray always and not to lose heart. He said, "In a certain city there was a judge who neither feared God nor had respect for people. In that city there was a widow who kept coming to him and saying, 'Grant me justice against my opponent.' For a while he refused; but later he said to himself, 'Though I have no fear of God and no respect for anyone, yet because this widow keeps bothering me, I will grant her justice, so that she may not wear me out by continually coming.' " And the Lord said, "Listen to what the unjust judge says. And will not God grant justice to his chosen ones who cry to him day and night? Will he delay long in helping them? I tell you, he will quickly grant justice to them. And yet, when the Son of Man comes, will he find faith on earth?" (Luke 18:1-8)

The closing question in that text has a haunting feel about it. Will God's people pray with such persistence, confident that it will change things? Will faith cut through the paradox between an all-knowing God and the possibility of change through prayer?

In his explanation of the Lord's Prayer, Martin Luther adds to this discussion when he writes about the phrase, "Your will be done." "God's will is done indeed without our prayers, but we pray in this petition that his will may be done among us also."

Typically of Luther, he does not dismiss either part of the paradox. On the one hand, the will of God will be done, but on the other hand, he affirms the role of prayer in seeking God's will being done in the particular situation of life that confronts a person.

Prayer changes things. Trust in the examples of faith and your own call to prayer to pursue the exciting journey of dialogue with God. It is in this confidence that you are called to the discipline of prayer in a ministry for yourself and the lives of others.

Intercessory Prayer

Beyond praying for your own needs, you are encouraged to pray for others. This ministry of prayer is a part of your call to be for others. It is a part of what is called the priesthood of all believers. As a Christian you are to be an active participant in the redeeming, caring, and consoling work of God. One of the vehicles of this ministry is prayer.

Intercession is the prayer you engage in for the sake of others. Throughout the letters of the apostle Paul and other New Testament writers requests are made for intercessory prayers.

Paul often requests such prayers for himself and other Christian workers. "Beloved, pray for us" (1 Thess. 5:25). Prayers are requested for government leaders:

> First of all, then, I urge that supplications, prayers, intercessions, and thanksgivings be made for everyone, for kings and all who are in high positions, so that we may lead a quiet and peaceable life in all godliness and dignity. (1 Tim. 2:1-2)

The apostle Paul often includes in his letters his intercessory prayers for those to whom he writes:

> For this reason, since the day we heard it, we have not ceased praying for you and asking that you may be filled with the knowledge of God's will in all spiritual wisdom and understanding. (Col. 1:9)

Prayer is a bond between all Christians. It is a way of affirming the Body of Christ. Prayer is a spiritual link in the realization of the connectedness we have with one another and how we may minister to each other. It is part of what constitutes the strength of the Christian community in its struggle against the forces of sin and evil. The Letter to the Ephesians urges you to fulfill this type of prayer ministry for the church today just as Paul urged it in his time:

> Pray in the Spirit at all times in every prayer and supplication. To that end keep alert and always persevere in supplication for all the saints. Pray also for me, so that when I speak, a message may be given to me to make known with boldness the mystery of the gospel, for which I am an ambassador in chains. Pray that I may declare it boldly, as I must speak. (Eph. 6:18-20)

There is no more important ministry in the church than the ministry of intercessory prayer. You have at hand a multitude of possibilities for prayer. Remember your pastor, other leaders in the church, and all those who share in your life in the congregation. The strength of fellowship and ministry of any congregation is strongly dependent upon this ministry of prayer on behalf of one another.

In many congregations there is a group that will gather on Sunday morning to pray specifically for the pastor and other leaders in the worship and for the congregation that will gather. Most congregations have a prayer-chain ministry in which those committed to intercessory prayer call each other with specific requests for prayer support. Family members can covenant together to pray daily for each other.

I am blessed with the knowledge that every day there are people praying for me. That awareness gives a thankful sense of belonging to the Body of Christ and of knowing God's guidance and protection.

Intercessory prayer can play another role in your Christian life. It can be the doorway through which opportunities for ministry may occur.

If you assume a ministry of intercession for someone, you may begin to experience a desire to become an active part of the answer to that prayer, if it is a situation in which your involvement can make a difference. Your loving words may soon become loving action.

The Letter of James reminds us that ministry is not only words but also deeds:

> If a brother or sister is naked and lacks daily food, and one of you says to them, "Go in peace; keep warm and eat your fill," and yet you do not supply their bodily needs, what is the good of that? (James 2:15-16)

In the same way, prayer can move beyond words to an act of compassion and caring in your own practice of intercession.

Intercessory prayer may hold yet another surprise for you, particularly if you are praying for a change in another person with whom you are involved.

Some years ago a pastor and his wife lived in a small town in a house next to the church. The house was on the edge of town and had the possibility of a beautiful view of the countryside from the dining room window. However, the view was blocked by a junk yard filled with wrecked cars and high weeds. It was also filled with rats. The owner of the junk yard had an unsavory reputation and was not an inviting individual. He was bitter and expressed his bitterness through excessive foul language.

The junk yard and its owner became an irritant to the pastor's wife, and she began to pray for a change in him and the removal of the junk yard. As she began to pray, however, a new thought entered her head. She was led to pray for herself that she might be given the gift of love and compassion for this man and the situation.

After the first night of praying in this new way, something startling happened. Early the next morning there was a knocking on the back door of the parsonage. There stood the junk yard owner. He held in his arms a large bag of vegetables from his garden, which he extended as an act of neighborliness and friendship.

Intercessory prayer may effect a change in you before it affects the one for whom you are praying. Often the key to effective intercessory prayer for another with whom you have a relationship is to be open to change within yourself. You may need to purify your motives and see the other with new eyes.

The importance of love as the motive for intercessory prayer should not be underestimated. The first petition of intercessory prayer may well be the request that your motive and desire come from the gift of God's love in your heart for the person for whom you are praying.

I believe that it is love that is the freeing power of intercessory prayer. Love allows you to let go and not to possess the person or situation. Love allows you to be willing for God to set things right, even if it means a change in you. Love frees others to make changes when they know they can give up their defensiveness.

The apostle Paul's description of God's self-giving love in 1 Corinthians is the kind of love intercessors should request:

Love is patient; love is kind; love is not envious or boastful or arrogant or rude. It does not insist on its own way; it is not irritable or resentful; it does not rejoice in wrongdoing, but rejoices in the truth. It bears all things, believes all things, hopes all things, endures all things. (1 Cor. 13:4-7)

49

Praying for change in others or on behalf of others in difficult situations is based on the truth that God cares.

Intercession for others allows you to be a channel of God's caring love. If you feel drawn to people's needs and sense a strong presence of God's compassion in you, then this type of prayer would be important for you to explore more deeply.

Prayer and Healing

In a survey taken in 1993, people said that they prayed most often about issues related to health. This is not such a surprising answer since our health, or a lack of it, affects us in so many ways. The presence of ill health can disrupt our emotions, economics, relationships, hope, and sense of self-worth. Disease is the point at which we realize our vulnerability and mortality and know how susceptible we are to having our lives disrupted or dramatically altered.

Even with all of the advances in physical medicine, psychiatry, and other forms of health care, our encounter with disease, illness, and sickness is still a major concern that has always been addressed by religious people in their prayers.

In Christianity, praying for and experiencing healing has been a part of the tradition of the church. It is rooted in the witness to healing found in the Bible. Early in Israel's history, just after the liberation and exodus from Egypt, God declared to them, "I am the Lord who heals you" (Exod. 15:26).

In addition, there are many stories of prayer and healing found in the lives of Moses, Isaiah, Elijah, and others in the Old Testament. These stories can be found in Numbers 21:4-9; Isaiah 38:1-8; 1 Kings 17:17-24; 2 Kings 5:1-14.

In the New Testament there are numerous stories of prayer and healing, particularly in the ministry of Jesus. In the Gospels of Matthew, Mark, and Luke, one-third of all the writing is related to the healing ministry of Jesus. In the gospel stories of Jesus you can see a broad healing ministry related to the forgiveness of sins, the curing of lepers, giving sight to the blind, making the lame walk, casting out demons, and raising the dead. Also, when Jesus sent out his disciples on missions to the surrounding area, he told them to preach, teach, and heal. This continued in the early church, as indicated by many stories in the book of Acts. These stories can be found in Acts 3:1-10; 9:10-19; 9:32-34; 19:11-12; 20:7-12; 28:7-10. The number of stories indicates that praying for healing was a normal practice in the early church.

Praying for healing has always been a part of the ministry of the church, but it has received varying degrees of attention in different periods of history. Today a revived interest in prayer and healing seems to be occurring. Denominations are publishing services of healing, and many congregations are providing opportunities for healing prayers in their public ministry. However, such prayers should not be confined to the worshiping congregation. They can be a part of every Christian's prayer life.

HEALING COMES FROM GOD

Healing is built into the creation. Our bodies naturally heal. Our souls and spirits stretch out toward healing. The process of healing is something of a mystery. It happens. Prayer can be a part of that process just as much as drugs, surgeries, counseling, and other medical care. We need to realize that our spiritual relationship with God is as real as our relationship to drugs, medical procedures, and counseling techniques. When we face the need for healing, God is an important factor in the process.

Numerous studies have shown that people who are prayed for by others heal more quickly than those for whom no one is praying. This in no way diminishes the importance of the medical practices of doctors and counselors, but the ministry of prayer adds the spiritual dimension to the process of healing.

The Bible uses the word *saved* not only for being made right with God, but also with reference to the healing of the body. The word for salvation used in the Bible is also the word that is translated *made well* or *whole*—the word used when describing the person who has consciously sought healing and is aware that the healing came from God. When disease or illness is overcome in persons without reference to a broad healing that affects the soul or spirit, the word *cure* is used. When one is cured, a disease and its symptoms are gone, but there is no awareness of a relationship to God in the curing. This implies a healing or wholeness that occurs when the cure is associated with a relationship with God.

51

In Luke's Gospel, Jesus encounters ten lepers. They appeal to him for healing. He tells them to go and show themselves to the priest. As they go they are cured. One comes back to thank Jesus and acknowledge the healing. Jesus says to the man, "Get up and go on your way; your faith has made you well" (Luke 17:19). A distinction is made between the nine who were cured and the one who was healed, or made well.

It is possible to be cured and not healed, according to the New Testament usage of language. Healing refers to the whole person being brought into balance; body, soul, and spirit are brought into a harmony in relationship with God. This does not mean that perfection has been attained. Perfection is not something that we will experience in this life. But we experience a sense of well-being when we are at peace with God and others that results in our restored health. The spiritual dimension of healing is important if we are to be healed and not just cured.

This became clear to me in an experience with a man who had requested prayers for healing for a severe heart condition for which he was receiving medical treatment. He was unable to walk more than a few feet without becoming completely exhausted. Two of us prayed for this man. Others had also prayed. I saw him two weeks after the prayer. He had walked to the church. He said that he was now walking to his senior center each day. However, he had come to share with me his disappointment that God had not cured him. No matter how much I tried to show him that he was better, he refused to see that anything had happened to him. He was not perfectly cured; therefore God had not done anything. He was unable to accept the cure he was experiencing as well as the healing he could receive by acknowledging God and giving thanks. The bitterness in his soul was blocking the process of wholeness or healing.

Prayer, as well as medicine, surgery, or counseling, has a role to play in your healing process. God is very much a part of the healing process, whether it is your body, emotions, mind, or spirit that needs attention.

GOD'S WILL AND HEALING

What is God's will regarding healing? Many people pray in a conditional way when it comes to healing. They will add, "If it be your will" when they pray. The Bible makes it clear that indeed it is God's will to heal. If we understand healing as the process of restoring all of your life, including your body, and renewing your relationship with God, then it is God's will to heal. God's will is salvation, wholeness, healing, restoration, and completion. The Bible shows God continually at work to restore that which is broken, whether it is a relationship, alienation from God, despair, or bones.

Effective prayer for healing begins with the conviction that it is in God's will that we be healed. Therefore, it is always appropriate to pray for healing. Will we always be cured? Not necessarily. Is it possible to understand why? Not necessarily. There are probably many reasons why some are cured and some are not. Such reasons may not be known to us. However, the basic conviction remains. God is at work drawing us ultimately to himself and to eternal life through the resurrection. In spite of those powers of darkness, brokenness, and sin that are allowed to be at work in the world, God will be there for us now, and in the end God will call us to share in the restoration of all things.

HEALING PRAYER AND FAITH

Faith is a component of healing prayer. In the New Testament stories of healing, faith is always present in some person involved in the event. Jesus acknowledges the faith that is present and often commends the faith of the one praying.

A striking example of this is the woman who came to Jesus because she was hemorrhaging. She had suffered with this for many years. She had spent all her money seeking a cure. When she heard about Jesus, she was determined to go to him. Realizing that she was unclean because of the blood as well as being a woman, she said to herself, "If I can just touch the hem of his garment I will be healed." In the midst of a crowd she did just that, and she was healed. Jesus said to her, "Take heart, daughter; your faith has made you well" (Matt. 9:20-23). Her faith—that is, her courage and trust to move beyond the boundaries set by society and her own mind—seemed to open her life to God's healing presence in Jesus.

God heals, and faith, the Holy Spirit's gift of courage to trust God, opens us up to receive whatever gift God will bestow. Faith

53

does not control the answer to prayer, but it is present when answers to prayer are given.

PRAYING FOR HEALING

Our most important healing is the forgiveness of sins. The source of healing is the restoration of our relationship with God. God's greatest act of self-revelation is Jesus Christ and the love portrayed through his self-giving on the cross. Raised from death by God, Jesus' resurrection becomes the sign of God's intent to restore all things.

You will find healing in your spirit through the prayer of confession and by receiving the forgiving word of God. In the first Letter of John we are encouraged to experience forgiveness by honestly confessing our sins. John writes, "If we confess our sins, God who is faithful and just will forgive us our sins and cleanse us from all unrighteousness" (1 John 1:9).

This fundamental reconciliation with God through Jesus Christ is the basic healing you need to come out from behind the fear, guilt, or shame that can create such destruction to your well-being. This is moving from death to life, from darkness to light.

In the Twelve-Step program of Alcoholics Anonymous, this is a fundamental step for a renewing process. There is an admission that one has lost control and is powerless over alcohol or whatever addiction is controlling one's life. The next steps move through a process of accountability and restoration.

Praying for healing is much the same. It begins with confession, a sharing with God of the brokenness and failure of one's life. Then, in receiving forgiveness, peace is restored within.

In the Letter of James we can see the relationship between forgiveness and healing:

Are any among you suffering? They should pray. Are any cheerful? They should sing songs of praise. Are any among you sick? They should call for the elders of the church and have them pray over them, anointing them with oil in the name of the Lord. The prayer of faith will save the sick, and the Lord will raise them up; and anyone who has committed sins will be forgiven. Therefore confess your sins to one another, and pray for one another, so that you may be healed. (James 5:13-16)

Being willing to open our whole life to ourselves and to God, even the most hidden parts of which we may be ashamed, is opening ourselves to God's healing grace.

After confession believe the word of forgiveness. God's forgiving love is like a cleansing of your whole self. Isaiah describes it this way: "Though your sins are like scarlet, they shall be like the snow; though they are red like crimson, they shall become like wool" (Isaiah 1:18).

Prayer includes receiving in faith what God answers to our requests. Listen to what God says. Prayer involves both speaking and listening, asking and receiving.

Praying for healing includes the past as well as the present. As more people have become aware of the wounding in childhood that has come from abuse or crises, they have felt a need to find healing for the emotional effects. Because God was present to all events in our life, even if God's presence was not acknowledged, those past hurts and the resulting emotions can be touched by God's healing power in Christ.

Pray for your wounded inner spirit. Ask God to bring to mind those memories that are causing problems. Visualize the scene and listen to Christ's healing words spoken to you.

God desires that we bring to him all of our needs and the needs we see in others. This is one of the purposes of prayer. There is nothing that is too awful or too trivial to bring to God. God desires our wholeness and well-being.

Praying as requesting can be summed up in this way: Come to God in humility and honest repentance, accepting God's forgiveness. Come to God in faith, expecting God to answer. Receive in faith God's answer. Give thanks for God's care and response.

There are some who find it hard to ask for anything. Their pride or individualism may be a barrier to reaching out. God may become a last resort for them. Doesn't it make more sense to begin with God as the first resource, rather than waiting to speak to God as the last hope?

This is an important lesson that you could pass on to children. Help them to think of God first whenever they have needs in their life. This does not mean that they should not learn responsibility for their initiative in solving problems, but they should be aware that God is always there to help them.

Whenever our children suffered a wound, illness, or difficult situation, prayer would be included in the response to the situation. Even when they were small and came with their little scratches and bumps, in addition to the Band-Aid and kiss to make it well, a healing prayer was offered. Both actions were important. They knew our love and compassion in the kiss, and knew God's care in the prayer.

With a lively spirit of prayer that is conscious of God in all moments of life, desire to put all things into God's presence, so that God's transforming power in Jesus Christ can make all things new.

3

Prayer of the Heart

A desire to be close to the reality of God's loving presence is a part of the journey of faith and a dimension of spirituality. In the prayer of the heart we seek to be still, silent, and focused on God. God is love; therefore to be in the presence of God is to be in the presence of love.

In this way we seek God for the sake of God alone. Our prayer is not motivated by the need to ask for or accomplish something. We seek only to know God's love as present and real.

Prayer of the heart is like bringing a vessel to a fountain. In order to be filled with water, the vessel must first be emptied; so, too, you must be separated from your attachments to things, ideas, fantasies, feelings, and concerns. Then, seeking a quiet, still place within, invite and wait for a sense of God's presence. This is more like *being* prayer than *doing* prayer.

Throughout the history of the Christian church there have been those who have felt a call to a separated, contemplative life. They have devoted themselves to a serious pursuit of experiencing God's presence in silence and solitude. These persons form a long line of mystics that stretches from the early church to the present time. They pursue a prayer life that seeks to know God in an inner experience of presence and love.

However, this form of prayer is not meant for them alone. Any Christian who feels drawn within can engage in the prayer that seeks God's presence in this inner quiet. In fact, this can be a form of prayer that any Christian may pursue.

Prayer of the heart was a part of Jesus' pattern of prayer. He often went off by himself to spend long periods in prayer, separating himself from others and the distractions and demands of the crowd.

> In the morning, while it was still very dark, he got up and went out to a deserted place, and there he prayed. (Mark 1:35)

> Now during those days he went out to the mountain to pray; and he spent the night in prayer to God. (Luke 6:12)

> Immediately he made the disciples get into the boat and go on ahead to the other side, while he dismissed the crowds. And after he had dismissed the crowds, he went up the mountain by himself to pray. (Matt. 14:22-23)

It may help to understand this type of prayer by thinking about a relationship you have with someone you love very much. If you and your loved one are always in the company of other people, you do not have a chance to enjoy being together in an intimate way, focused on each other. Your attention will be drawn to the others around you. If this were to happen most of the time, you would not be able to develop a very deep relationship. If you desire an intimate relationship with God, times set apart for quietness in God's presence are important.

Jesus encouraged his disciples to set aside time for this type of prayer as well. In Mark's Gospel Jesus invites his disciples to come away with him and rest in a desert place (Mark 6:31). Like Jesus himself, they are invited to come away from distraction and focus on God.

The word *rest* in the Bible has a special meaning; it means to be in the presence of God without distraction. Among the Jewish people the Sabbath rest was the setting aside of one day in the week to pay attention to God. The writer of the Letter to the Hebrews speaks of entering God's rest as being in God's eternal presence (Heb. 4:10-11).

Several Old Testament examples point to this aspect of prayer as important to our relationship with God:

> Be still, and know that I am God. (Ps. 46:10)

Psalm 42 is often prayed by those who feel a great desire to know God intimately within: "As a deer longs for flowing streams, so my soul longs for you, O God" (Ps. 42:1).

The prophet Elijah had run away in despair, thinking that he alone remained faithful in Israel. He was hiding in a cave in the mountains. The Lord came to him and said that he was about to pass by. Elijah went outside and the following scene occurred:

> Now there was a great wind, so strong that it was splitting mountains and breaking rocks in pieces before the Lord, but the Lord was not in the wind; and after the wind an earthquake, but the Lord was not in the earthquake; and after the earthquake a fire, but the Lord was not in the fire; and after the fire a sound of sheer silence. When Elijah heard it, he wrapped his face in his mantle and went out and stood at the entrance of the cave. Then there came a voice to him that said, "What are you doing here, Elijah?" (1 Kings 19:11-13)

The writings of the mystics of the past show evidence of the way in which the prayer of the heart—this inner journey to know God's presence within—strengthens and provides growth for the spiritual journey. Their descriptions of this type of prayer contain clues for pursuing a deepening prayer journey for yourself.

Today there seems to be a stirring in the souls of many seekers wanting a deeper intimacy with God. This stirring has caused many to seek this prayer experience in Eastern religions, New Age experiments, and revived ancient religious practices.

Because they have not heard or seen this practiced in the church, many assume that this form of prayer is not a part of the Christian tradition. However, this tradition does exist within the Christian church and can provide ways of practicing this form of prayer that are consistent with the Christian understanding of God and the way God relates to us in Jesus and the Holy Spirit.

As a teenager growing up in a small Lutheran church in South Chicago, I attended the midweek prayer meeting at our church. It was a small group, all adults except for myself. The meeting consisted of Bible readings, sharing about the way in which God had been at work in people's lives that week, and an extended prayer time, most of which was silence.

What drew me to that meeting week after week? It was the prayer time, especially the silence. A wonderful world within was opened to me. In that silence I began to experience a sense of God's presence that was different from anything else I had known. In that shared quiet time I began a journey to a calm center where I came to experience an embracing of God's overwhelming love for me.

Silence, stillness, and solitude—these three words describe the process of moving inward. Silence involves eliminating distractions from the outer world. Stillness refers to the inner calm and avoidance of distractions from within. Solitude is the place of coming to ourselves without distraction so that the still, small voice of God can be heard and the loving presence of God experienced—important because of what we face within ourselves and in the world around us.

It should be no secret to any of us that our lives are filled with ourselves. Our desires, needs, thoughts, feelings, and experiences take up most of the room in our awareness and most of the time of each day. This is particularly true if our lives are filled with great desires that have a compulsive hold on us. In the prayer of the heart we attempt to empty ourselves of the many distractions that tend to focus our attention on these compulsive thoughts. Many of these addictive patterns are focused on negative responses in our lives—fear, anxiety, anger, or pride. These are disruptive and debilitating, consume vast amounts of energy, and divert us from being able to focus on God.

Another negative aspect is the way we have taken so many illusions into our lives. In order to defend ourselves or give meaning to life, we often grasp at that which is false. Often we are unaware of these illusions and assume that they are the way to live in order to protect ourselves and make the good life happen. However, this is not the case. There are many examples of people who have come to a new realization and discovered in their lives that they had been following a false path.

The great theologian Augustine spent the early years of his life with the pursuit of pleasure as his main goal. When Augustine was finally converted to Christianity, his path moved in a new direction. He began to live out of God's direction for his life and not out of the compulsive desires of the flesh.

60

In the New Testament, we can read a similar story in the life of Peter. He was characterized by much bravado and impulsive courage as he followed Jesus. He was quick to use his strength to take charge and make rash statements about the depth of his love and commitment to Jesus. He was the one who would never run away in a time of crisis. When he did deny Jesus three times at the time of the crucifixion, he went out and wept bitterly. From that point on, his life changed. His ego was finally confronted by the reality that he was more afraid of dying than he realized. He ran to save his own life, but he was not yet ready to lay down his life for his friend. He had been living under an illusion. When he comes into a new understanding, he becomes a new person— fit for apostolic service, filled with the love of God and the Holy Spirit, and journeying on a different road.

The basic task for all of us, then, is to face up to the question, Am I walking a road built on an illusion, or am I clearly seeing who I truly am and what God has created me to be? Thus the prayer of the heart serves an important purpose on our Christian journey. It is part of the process of self-emptying and disillusioning that brings our life into line with the purposes of God.

If we are so focused on ourselves, how does God get in? There are various forms of prayer that accomplish this purpose. The following descriptions of prayer for the inner journey will provide you with an overview of Christian practices.

Several traditions exist in contemplative prayer. Some have focused on what is called the apophatic form of prayer. The emphasis in this prayer form is on the unknowable nature of God. God is so different from us that we cannot with the mind know God as God exists in divine nature. We must leave behind all metaphors, images, and words to seek an inner space devoid of everything so that we may encounter God who cannot be known through any created means, but only in naked love.

Another tradition of contemplative prayer is called the kataphatic. Here the emphasis is on meeting the God in whose image we have been created. The journey inward moves with images, metaphors, and words that grow out of the revelation of God in creation and Scripture. This tradition seeks to meet God as God can be known and experienced through God's gracious presence and love. Most Christians probably practice the kataphatic form of contemplative prayer.

The apophatic tradition can be found in *The Cloud Of Unknowing*, which is listed in the book list at the end of this book. The kataphatic tradition can be explored in the writings of Teresa of Avila and Ignatius Loyola, among others.

I remember singing a gospel song often in my youth that describes what happens in contemplative prayer.

Open mine eyes, O Lord; open mine eyes.
Into my darkened heart let Thy light arise.
Show me myself, O Lord. Show me Thyself, O Lord.
Show me Thy truth, O Lord. Open mine Eyes.[2]

In silence, stillness, and solitude God will be perceived and God's truth will be expressed. You may begin to see yourself more clearly—your weaknesses, strengths, illusions, and commitments. You will come to see Christ more clearly—the beauty, joy, and love he brings you. You will see God's truth more clearly—God's will and purpose for your life.

Contemplative prayer has been criticized by some as an escape from what they would call the real, outer world. However, this is not borne out by looking at the lives of those who seriously practice contemplative prayer.

Teresa of Avila ran several convents and reorganized her whole order while being a contemplative. Thomas Merton, a Trappist monk, was sensitive to the political and social concerns of our day as well as the author of many volumes. Martin Luther, a man of deep prayer, said that the busier he got the more time he had to take for prayer. The busiest homemaker, executive, farmer, pastor, student, or salesperson can practice contemplative prayer.

If you think contemplative prayer means abandoning the world, as critics have said, that is not so. Contemplative prayer actually is a means by which you can become motivated toward action, empowered by love, and kept humble. If you encounter God's love in contemplative prayer, that love will, in turn, move your life toward your neighbor.

The prophet Isaiah described a personal experience in which he encountered God in a vision. This experience illuminates some of the elements of contemplative prayer. Isaiah saw himself in the temple. Suddenly God was present in an awe-inspiring vision.

I saw the Lord sitting on a throne, high and lofty; and the hem of his robe filled the temple. Seraphs were in attendance above him; each had six wings; with two they covered their faces, and with two they covered their feet, and with two they flew. (Isa. 6:1-2)

The holiness of God was being proclaimed by the seraphs, and the threshold shook while smoke filled the temple. Confronting the holiness of God, Isaiah immediately became aware of his own sinfulness and weakness. He was caught knowing his own sin, and yet he saw God. His lips were touched with a burning coal and he was cleansed from his sin. The voice of God called out, "Whom shall I send, and who will go for us?" Isaiah responded, "Here am I, send me." Called within by God, Isaiah experienced an encounter with holiness, a vision of his own unworthiness, a cleansing, and a call to serve God and the people.

Add to the experience of Isaiah the New Testament experience of intimate love from God in Christ and you have the elements of the inner experience of the prayer of the heart.

The inner journey of prayer has always been a part of the prayer experience of God's people. If your religious experience is limited to external rites or only to that which is rational and material, a large portion of being in Christ and experiencing God's love will be missing. In Ephesians the image of this heart knowledge is made clear:

I pray that God of our Lord Jesus Christ, the Father of glory, may give you a spirit of wisdom and revelation as you come to know him, so that, with the eyes of your heart enlightened, you may know what is the hope to which he has called you, what are the riches of his glorious inheritance among the saints, and what is the immeasurable greatness of his power for us who believe, according to the working of his great power. (Eph. 1:17-19)

With his imagery of "the eyes of the heart," the writer is clearly pointing to a real inner experience within the soul and spirit. It is this experience that the prayer of the heart seeks to find.

An Experience of Contemplative Prayer

You could begin an exploration of contemplative prayer by setting aside some time each day. Begin with a minimum of ten minutes and gradually extend the time.

When you begin, find a comfortable place in the room and a comfortable position for your body. Close your eyes, relax, and let the cares and concerns of the day leave you.

Become aware of your breath. Notice its rhythm as it moves in and out of your lungs. You may focus on your breathing as a way of clearing your mind of distractions. Mentally pray for God to bless you in this time of quiet and to grant you an experience of God's love and presence. Let yourself relax and rest in the quiet. If mental distractions come, let them pass by. Do not resist them. Return to an awareness of your breath and its rhythm.

You may want to use an image of Christ or a particular Bible verse to focus on in your quiet time. Try not to control what you are going to think or feel. Be in a receptive mode in your silent time. Try not to worry whether or not you are doing it correctly. If you feel called to the quiet, begin to try several different forms of contemplative prayer.

Not everyone finds contemplative prayer easy. Some temperaments find it difficult to relate to silence and inwardness. However, there is value for everyone in this type of prayer. Do not think you have to do it just like someone else. Experiment with various ways.

Be aware of the following cautions:

- Do not assume that every voice you hear within comes from God.
- If you have an experience of God's nearness and love, cherish and learn from it. It may be wise not to share it immediately with others.
- Expect to become aware of things about yourself that should change.
- Change will come slowly.
- Stay close to Christ in your reflection and prayer.
- Test all your experiences against the Bible.
- Pray for humility.

Centering Prayer

A beginning method of exploring contemplation is centering prayer. The object of centering prayer is to be able to focus on one thing—to center oneself on one particular image or sound so that all else is put aside.

When we seek that empty place, the place of solitude, we need to overcome a few distractions. One of these is the outside world, the world we experience with our senses. It helps to close the eyes and block out the sight of the outer world.

Position yourself to receive the sense or experience of God's loving presence. Assume a listening posture in order that God may speak through the still, small voice within. Sit comfortably in a chair with legs uncrossed, hands resting loosely on your lap, the back straight, and head held erect. Do not force your breathing, just let it flow naturally. You will not get uncomfortable being in one position if your body is relaxed.

The next task is more difficult—finding silence within, coming to the center of yourself in quiet and solitude. As soon as you relax and turn off the outside world, you will become very aware of your multitudinous thoughts, feelings, and inner awareness. John Donne describes his struggle in these words spoken in a funeral sermon on Dec. 12, 1626:

I throw myself down in my Chamber, and I call in, and invite God, and his Angels thither, and when they are there, I neglect God and his Angels, for the noise of a fly, for the rattling of a coach, for the whining of a door.

The first temptation is to resist such thoughts. However, a better strategy is to acknowledge these thoughts and feelings and let them pass right on by. Do not resist them or dwell on them. Rather, and this is the main point of centering prayer, have a prayer word or phrase on which you can focus so that you can return to the center. If you are interrupted by thoughts, return to your image or word.

Examples of these words or phrases are Jesus Christ, Abba, Holy Spirit, Lord, have mercy, or whatever you choose as your particular centering word.

For an in-depth description of centering prayer refer to the book *Centering Prayer* by Basil Pennington, listed in the recommended reading section of this book.

Practicing the Presence of God

Brother Lawrence, a humble monk who served in the kitchen of a monastery at the most menial tasks, came upon a truth for his life that has opened the door for many others to a simple way to pray in the midst of life. After his conversion and an experience in which he desired to give over every moment to God, Brother Lawrence set out to find the way in which God would be present to him no matter what he was doing. In the midst of his work, leisure, and worship he tried to hold on to one primary thought: God is present.

It took him many years to reach a point where he found a profound inner peace through this practice. It is no easy task to overcome the weakness of the flesh and the distractions of life. As we all know, many things fill our minds and cry out for our attention. God can be crowded out by all of that.

Brother Lawrence has been a teacher to many who have sought a practical, simple way in which to be conscious of God in all activities and to live centered in the peace and serenity that God's presence brings.

Brother Lawrence's motivation was not an attempt to earn God's favor or just to find serenity. He understood clearly the way in which God's grace comes freely in Christ, bringing forgiveness and holiness. His desire for practicing the presence of God was to find his whole life absorbed in the gracious and loving presence of God.

This is not a complicated way of praying and is not dependent on any certain form. It requires only that you remain aware of and pay attention to God's presence in each moment. For those who are practically minded and find it difficult to practice a disciplined form of contemplation, this form of prayer of the heart may serve you well.

Exploring how others have prayed and reading about the benefits it has brought to their lives is worthwhile. But sooner or later, you need to try it on your own. A helpful way to grow in the use of contemplative prayer is to set aside specific periods of time. Commit these times to silence and find a place where you will not be easily disturbed.

You can set aside a time each day. Make your prayer period long enough so that your prayer is not rushed. It is better not to have to force yourself into solitude in a hurried manner. Do not think of the time in silence according to clock time. Judge the time spent in solitude according to its quality and purpose. Some days this may be fifteen minutes. Other days it may be an hour.

Let go of the time and space factors in controlling contemplative prayer. This is part of what you want to let go in the prayer of the heart. You place yourself before God and wait patiently for God to fill the moments with love and presence.

Some people adopt the discipline of a longer silent prayer period one day a week. It is like a Sabbath rest. The time is filled with contemplative prayer, journaling, Scripture reflection, and expressing prayer through drawing, clay, or dance. This becomes a rich time of renewal of the relationship you have with your Lord.

There are many retreat or prayer centers that will provide space and hospitality for silent retreats. They may last for a few hours or a few days. An annual three day silent retreat is a pattern many follow.

I remember a woman whose whole prayer life, and subsequently her life, changed when she attended a three-day silent retreat I was leading. She discovered the transforming power of silence and contemplative prayer. As she journaled her experiences, she realized in a fresh way how God is willing and able to speak to us within and bring insight and wisdom for self-understanding.

If you feel uncomfortable or fearful exploring the prayer of the heart on your own, seek out a spiritual director or use the program of guided retreats at a prayer center.

4

Prayer as Enlightenment

To pray is to have your mind, heart, and senses opened to God and to life around you. Prayer is not an escape from facing who you are or what you are called to be and to do. Prayer is part of that process of becoming—the unfolding of your life in a world God has created and the directing of your life with the purpose God has in mind.

Prayer is not a substitute for struggling and learning to unravel the mystery of who you are or your life's purpose. Prayer is entering into the struggle. It is one of the tools a Christian can use in the search for enlightenment and the process of discernment. Prayer is a particular way of listening to God, the Scriptures, your Christian community, and the whole human community around you.

A form of prayer that focuses on a particular issue or question in order to gain wisdom is called meditation. If contemplation is seeking to experience the heart of God, meditation is seeking to know the mind of God. When you pray focusing on a particular issue, you try to hear what God has to say. It may have to do with understanding yourself, finding a direction in which to move, or discerning God's will. The reflection could focus on understanding a passage of Scripture, choices that have to be made, the next steps in spiritual growth, or removing obstacles in your path.

Meditation and contemplation share much of the same method. Seek a silence in which distractions can be removed. Look for a place within in which God may speak to the issue with which you are struggling. You may ponder the Bible, spiritual advice of others, readings, or just wait for an inner illumination.

The wisdom that is sought in meditation is not just knowledge in and of itself. It is wisdom in the sense of knowing how to apply knowledge in a practical and direct way to your life.

Psalm 119 describes the function of the wisdom of God's teaching: "Your word is a lamp to my feet and a light to my path" (Ps. 119:105). The word of God becomes wisdom when it directs you on your journey. Wisdom gained from God's teaching directs your decisions, self-understanding, actions, and goals. This happens when your life is seen through the lens of God's word.

If you study the Scriptures only to understand them objectively, the personal nature of Christ in the Word can be lost. Rather than looking at the Scriptures as something to be taken into a laboratory to be put under a microscope, think of the Scriptures as the microscope examining yourself. Or as the Letter of James describes it, think of the word as a mirror in which you are revealed to yourself. His caution is, don't see the image and walk away forgetting what you saw. Rather, see the image of yourself and then go and do what it directs. The point is, you are not just to understand the Bible intellectually, although that is important, but ultimately the Word is meant to effect your whole life by its presence within you.

Meditation does bring enlightenment or illumination. The inner reflection that takes place in meditation is a bridge between a question, decision, or concern in your life and God's direction about that concern. You want to perceive God's word as it applies to your life. Like a midwife, the Holy Spirit uses meditative prayer to bring to birth in your life the life and the light that is Jesus.

Meditation is nurtured by the Word of God that is Jesus Christ. That Word is present in the Bible, in the sacraments, in the fellowship of Christians, and in the prayerful silence within. These are not separate words. In whatever form that Word appears it is the same Word—Jesus Christ.

In the Old Testament, the psalmist writes a beautiful hymn about God's teaching. Psalm 119 is a devotional meditation on God's law—God's word to his people. Several verses in this psalm describe how this teaching inspires praise, thanksgiving, and reflection.

I find my delight in your commandments,
    because I love them.
I revere your commandments, which I love,
    and I will meditate on your statutes. (Ps. 119:47-48)

Dietrich Bonhoeffer, a theologian who lived in Germany during the 1930s, wrote a book on Christian community and devoted much of it to prayer and the presence of God's Word in the community of faith. He writes:

We are silent at the beginning of the day because God should have the first word, and we are silent before going to sleep because the last word also belongs to God. We keep silence solely for the sake of the Word. This stillness before the Word will exert its influence upon the whole day.[3]

In meditation you may take with you into silence a portion of Scripture to reflect on how it relates to your life. You may enter the silent reflection bringing a question, desiring to hear the answer come to you in the quiet. You may also bring the advice or counsel of friends into your quiet time to discern its truth for you.

One way to reflect upon Scripture or other material is to approach it prayerfully. Begin with prayer, seeking to put yourself into a receptive mode. Slowly read the text, perhaps more than once. Think about its meaning and notice any particular phrases or images from the text that catch your attention. Center yourself in quietness and stillness and keep the Word before your mind. Be together with the Word, focused and attentive to it. Examine it from many sides. Write down insights and understandings that come to you. Close your meditation with a prayer of thanksgiving.

Ignatius Loyola taught a method of Scripture reflection that uses the senses and imagination in the meditative process. This works particularly well for the stories of the gospel or Old Testament. Read the passage noticing all the persons involved, where it took place, and any other descriptive words in the story. Take the scene with you into silence and let the scene begin to be played out in your imagination. See the people, feel the breeze, smell the flowers, notice people's reactions. Let the scene be rebuilt within you and speak to you as you find yourself in the middle of the story.

Since Jesus Christ is the way, the path you seek to follow, enlightenment will come as you meditate on Jesus' life and teaching. Your purpose in focusing on Jesus is to enable you to think and respond biblically with your life. You are seeking the mind of Christ within yourself.

In his Letter to the Colossians, the apostle Paul writes what could be understood as the goal of Christian enlightenment, the path illumined by the presence of God's Word within you:

As God's chosen ones, holy and beloved, clothe yourselves with compassion, kindness, meekness, and patience. Bear with one another and, if anyone has a complaint against another, forgive each other; just as the Lord has forgiven you, so you also must forgive. Above all, clothe yourselves with love, which binds everything together in perfect harmony. . . . Let the word of Christ dwell in you richly; teach and admonish one another in all wisdom; and with gratitude in your hearts sing psalms, hymns, and spiritual songs to God. And whatever you do, in word or deed, do everything in the name of the Lord Jesus, giving thanks to God the Father through him. (Col. 3:12-14, 16-17)

Another aspect of meditative prayer that is important to Christians is discernment—the process of discovering God's will in a particular situation and being persuaded to follow it.

In addition to listing the positive and negative results of a certain action in attempting to make a decision, you can also take the question to God in reflective prayer. Enter your silent time bringing your question with you, and wait for God to speak to you about it. The question may be answered quite directly through a sense of peace that comes with a certain decision. Or certain answers may be eliminated by the negative response you feel. As you meditate in a discerning process, expect that God may first help you clarify or challenge your motives. Be prepared to be changed. Be prepared, also, to wait. Often the discernment process will take time.

Another dimension of the discernment process is the practice of praying with others about the decision. You can enlist friends to pray with you in a meditative way. This provides both support and confirmation of a decision you may reach. Jesus indicated that praying with others would enhance this discerning process.

> Again, truly I tell you, if two of you agree on earth about anything you ask, it will be done for you by my Father in heaven. For where two or three are gathered in my name, I am there among them. (Matt. 18:19-20)

Including others in the discerning process allows them to confirm or deny your own leanings. The important element here is not the quantity of people increasing the effectiveness of prayer but the issue of a consensus among believers confirming that the action is God's will.

Jesus' three-hour meditation in the Garden of Gethsemane before his crucifixion illuminates another aspect of prayer and the discerning process. Jesus knew God's will for him.

As he faced the cross, he sought to discern whether this was the only way. The prospect of the weight of the world's sin and the confrontation with death as the sin-bearer who himself knew no sin threw him into an agony. Jesus was seeking confidence that this was truly God's path for him and strength to walk in that path.

You may come to know God's will in prayer but then face obstacles in carrying it out. Fear, anxiety, pride, or loss of possessions may paralyze you. You may have to spend time in deep prayer with God, seeking God's help to overcome these obstacles before you can act on what you have discovered as God's will for you.

The writer of Psalm 119 describes how the prayer of meditation on God's teaching brings a depth of wisdom and discernment:

Oh, how I love your law!
It is my meditation all day long.
Your commandment makes me wiser than my enemies,
for it is always with me.
I have more understanding than all my teachers,
for your decrees are my meditation.
I understand more than the aged,
for I keep your precepts.
I hold back my feet from every evil way,

in order to keep your word. (Ps. 119:97-101)

Linking God's word with meditation is an important part of the Christian's journey to wisdom. Wisdom is a gift God offers us to enable us to live our life in accordance with God's will. The Bible encourages us to pray for wisdom:

If any of you is lacking in wisdom, ask God, who gives to all generously and ungrudgingly, and it will be given you. But ask in faith, never doubting, for the one who doubts is like a wave of the sea, driven and tossed by the wind. (James 1:5-6)

What you allow your mind to dwell on shapes much of your life. You may, from time to time, find yourself struggling with a particular issue in your life. Your active, petitioning prayer may be asking God to change you, but your meditation or reflection time is focused on the very thing you want removed. Moral struggles against lust, gambling, laziness, or envy may be lost because they are the object of all of your thoughts, fantasies, or inward reflection. Too many Christians may focus their verbal prayers, that take a few moments, on moral goodness, but spend hours of inward reflection on negative thoughts and material.

In Philippians the apostle Paul gives wise counsel about focusing your thoughts on that which will edify your life:

Finally, beloved, whatever is true, whatever is honorable, whatever is just, whatever is pure, whatever is pleasing, whatever is commendable, if there is any excellence and if there is anything worthy of praise, think about these things. (Phil. 4:8)

There is a caution about meditative practices. Be careful to distinguish between fantasy and prayer images, between daydreaming and prayerful meditation.

Fantasy is an inward flight of wish-fulfillment, desire, or escape from a harsh reality. Usually it is not rooted in a promise of God or based on the reality of your life. Often it may be an expression of a desire rooted in the flesh as opposed to the spirit. It tends to be self-centered and ego gratifying. Not all fantasy is bad; however, it should not be confused with prayer.

Meditative prayer uses the imagination as a God-given part of who you are. In prayer the imagination is inspired by the Spirit to give form to the prayer and allows for visualization of the subject of the meditation.

Imagination, then, becomes an instrument of the Spirit to enhance your edification and knowledge. Meditative prayer is a part of your journey to holiness and sanctification and not a part of fantasies that will be destructive to your moral character and behavior.

As you move forward in your prayer journey, meditation will be an important part of your growth. It will provide a positive means of enlightenment by the word of God for your life. Your discernment of God's will for yourself will be strengthened, and you will be edified for a life that reflects holiness and wholesomeness.

5

Prayer as Complaint

P rayer has political and social dimensions. In the give-and-take of society, in the daily comings and goings of people, suffering and injustice become very evident. There are victims and victimizers. People win and people lose. Some control and others are controlled. Power is misused. Violence breaks lives apart. People are rejected and marginalized.

An ancient prayer of the church has been spoken by people of every generation who have become troddened down, overcome, caused to suffer unjustly, and abandoned.

Kyrie eleison. Lord, have mercy! This prayer cries out the human pain and anguish to God. It is spoken by those in need and by those who want to identify with the suffering ones. "Lord, have mercy" is the prayer that tells God that the situation is bigger than what you can handle. It is the honest expression of complaint to God that things are not right and are too overwhelming for you to change.

It is important to pray congruently with your feelings and the human situation. Too often Christians have been unwilling to share their pain, sorrow, or anger. They feared that they would be judged as not Christian enough if they were suffering. This notion is based on the assumption that faithful Christians never suffer and should always be smiling. It is true that Christians have a strong support in God and a knowledge of God's never-ending care, yet the cries of God's people in the Bible are unmistakably clear. They honestly offer up their pain, their sorrow, and their anger at injustice. You are not less a Christian if you experience sorrow, pain, anguish, or righteous indignation.

God heard the cries of his people suffering in Egypt. Jesus heard the cry for mercy from blind Bartimaeus. God hears and honors the prayers of complaint and the crying out of the heart. Perhaps one of the reasons salvation or healing is not experienced is that those suffering pain, sorrow, or righteous indignation will not admit it or express it. A healthy sob or wail is often the beginning of healing and transformation.

I was teaching at a weekend retreat. The opening sentence of a talk I gave at a worship service at this retreat referred to being abandoned. The word had barely left my mouth when a woman in the front row began to sob, and then to wail. In speaking with her after the service I discovered that her deepest pain had to do with a sense of abandonment, but she never allowed herself to think that word or express her pain. At the moment I used the word, the pain would be held no longer. It burst from her. It was a true heart-cry. That prayer of pain, bursting forth like a broken boil, began a healing process that had been hindered by the failure to offer that pain to God and others in prayer.

Loneliness is a mark of our time. Many lack intimacy with others and God. It is often glazed over with a veneer of light-heartedness and manufactured joy.

God's invitation to pray is an invitation to intimacy. God seeks to reach across the abyss that often separates and to unite with you in an experience of deep fellowship and belonging. If you resist or suppress the pain, anger, or loneliness you feel, you cannot respond to invitations to intimacy. The cry-of-the-heart prayer is the giving over of yourself to God's justice and mercy. Such prayer is part of the process of dealing with the loss, despair, or hurt. It is giving voice to your realization of what is happening to you, the cry of reality.

The Cry of Righteous Anger

Injustice provokes anger. When you are aware of others or yourself being treated unjustly, and you know that you are being victimized, the hurt and frustration turn to anger. These feelings can be repressed, or they can be allowed to turn to vengeance.

Jesus spoke about loving your enemies and praying for them. He offers another way to respond to injustice. Rather than letting anger become violence directed by self-pity and revenge, he directs you to undergird whatever prophetic word or action you may take with prayer. Prayer that is rooted in love for your enemy directs prophetic change in accordance with God's heart for justice and freedom. It is no longer just a personal, ego-driven campaign to get even or to hurt someone.

Much of today's violence on the streets demonstrates anger and frustration at work. It does not create a new society or bring resolution to social problems.

Jesus gave voice to his frustrations over the people who refused to see in him God's gift of life and hope. "How often have I desired to gather your children together as a hen gathers her brood under her wings, and you were not willing!" (Matt. 23:37b). His message contained warnings about such rejection, but he did not set out on a personal vendetta to destroy his enemies. When he was arrested in the Garden of Gethsemane, he told his disciples to put up their swords. The issue was much larger than Jesus' personal safety or his personal vindication. The prayer that undergirds prophetic vision, speech, and action is the prayer that allows God to shape our response in view of God's vindication and not our own.

In our own time we have models like Gandhi and Martin Luther King Jr. who rooted their prophetic response to injustice in a deep spirituality that stayed connected to God's purposes and God's role as the vindicator of his people. By action and teaching they tried to keep the struggle from becoming merely personal vengeance or irresponsible violence.

As a Christian you give voice to your personal feelings but then seek to channel your prayer and response according to God's justice and in a spirit of love and transformation.

A homely illustration of this is the case of the man who is rudely awakened by some disparaging words from his wife. He buries his response within, but all day long he spreads his anger out into the world by his rude treatment of the bus driver, coworkers, and the family dog. By repressing his frustration and anger he does not solve the problem: instead he indiscriminately takes it out on others who do not deserve it, and in the end he finds no true satisfaction or resolution.

Give voice to the cry in your heart, direct your ways toward love of your enemies, and follow God's lead in seeking justice and freedom.

The cry of the heart in righteous anger may refer to someone else's situation rather than your own. Compassion for situations of injustice, whether for one person or a group in society, may cause you to want to respond with some kind of action. Again it is important that it be rooted in prayer so that you are in touch with a motivation that is not just an emotional response but instead grows from understanding God's will.

History reveals that many times revolutions that began with a desire to reform society and seek justice only supplanted one unjust government with another. The foundation of justice and its expression were not explored or developed so that a true change could happen. Power has a tendency to corrupt and may not bring justice if it is not wedded to love.

The prophet Jonah found himself angry with God when the people of Nineveh repented and God withheld judgment. Jonah's anger was rooted in his self-concern that he be seen as a prophet announcing destruction. God's mercy embarrassed him. As a prophet he was no longer on God's mission but his own self-vindication. He had lost sight of the power of God's word to bring change and had focused only on what they deserved—destruction.

Praying about justice, like all prayer, means offering the situation up to God, following God's lead in taking action, and then seeing how God will take care of it. The results of prayer are always in God's hands, God's time, and through God's means.

When you are moved by compassion to cry out in righteous anger the next steps are often steps of personal involvement. Very often this type of prayer becomes a prelude to action. The questions that follow the heart-cry for justice are, What can I do about it? How can I make a difference? Where do I go from here? Am I contributing to the problem? These questions may lead you to continue your prayer in another form.

Prayer is not a substitute for what God may want to do through you to answer the prayer and transform the situation.

The cry of the heart for justice can lead to a searching out of God's will in the situation. The prayer may continue by your involvement in political or social action to transform the problem. In addition, you may find ways of bringing encouragement to those suffering by living in solidarity with them. All of the above are a part of prayer—thoughts, feelings, words, and actions.

The Cry for Mercy

There are many situations in life in which you may find yourself in great need of help from beyond your resources or strength. Being willing to ask for such help can be a problem. Sometimes you may feel that you deserve what is happening to you and take it as punishment for your guilt. Many people feel that they have no right to expect mercy and have to pay for their sins. They may have been shamed to the point where they dare not ask for help. At other times you may feel threatened by any show of weakness or vulnerability and will go it alone. Such stoicism may rob you of the help you really need.

The gospel stories of Jesus encourage you to believe in the mercy God offers you. God invites you to come out from behind shame, guilt, and pride to stand in the light of God's mercy.

Can you imagine the wonderful surprise when a homeless, rejected, dying person on the streets of Calcutta is tenderly picked up and carried to a clean bed and surrounded by loving, touching people? Mother Teresa and her workers embody for hundreds what it means to have the cry for mercy heard. She lives out what we read in the pages of the New Testament, Jesus' acceptance and mercy offered to those bowed down with shame and guilt. "Lord, have mercy" is the cry on the lips of the blind, the woman pleading for her daughter, and so many others. Encouraged by Jesus' invitation to come to him, all who came found themselves accepted and helped, no matter what they had done or who they were.

One day a group of leaders brought a woman to Jesus who had been caught committing adultery. By law she could be stoned. We do not know what was in the mind of the woman. No doubt she thought her life had come to an end. She was guilty and probably expected a harsh judgment, even from Jesus. But lo and behold, she heard words of forgiveness. Mercy instead of judgment.

Again, the cry of the heart is the beginning of transformation. The cry for mercy, the humility to ask for help beyond yourself, opens the door to change.

This type of prayer is an expression of what is in the heart. It is not meant to be an explanation or rationalization. You just cry out for mercy. There is no need to explain or to justify yourself: simply trusting in God's mercy, you cry to God from the heart.

Jesus told this parable as an example of the cry of the heart and its use in seeking mercy:

> Two men went up to the temple to pray, one a Pharisee and the other a tax collector. The Pharisee, standing by himself, was praying thus, "God, I thank you that I am not like other people: thieves, rogues, adulterers, or even like this tax collector. I fast twice a week; I give a tenth of all my income." But the tax collector, standing far off, would not even look up to heaven, but was beating his breast and saying, "God, be merciful to me a sinner!" I tell you, this man went down to his home justified rather than the other. (Luke 18:10-14)

The Pharisee covered over his guilt with rationalization and comparison. He was not able to receive mercy because he felt no need for mercy in his heart. The tax collector had a simple cry from the heart. It was what he truly felt, and in no way did he try to dismiss it or mask it. He left with a clean heart. The other, because of his repressed guilt, left with only a more hardened heart, able neither to receive nor give mercy. He was more apt to judge than to forgive, because he refused to acknowledge what was in his heart.

The Cry of Abandonment

The pain of rejection and abandonment is another of the deep heart cries of many people. Whether it is a childhood memory or a more recent experience, such moments in your life create a deep ache.

As humans we have been made for fellowship and relationship. Loneliness denies a meaningful part of what it is to be a human being. Experiences of abandonment and rejection can create a bitter and cynical spirit if allowed to fester within. Trust becomes difficult for anyone who has been abandoned. Often such experiences are denied by the person and not allowed to be expressed.

80

Such repression stifles a healthy prayer relationship with God because of the fear of being abandoned by God as well as by others.

In our contemporary society there are a large number of persons who have experienced a variety of abusive situations. These experiences are like abandonment issues. Trust has broken down and a separation has taken place with persons who had been loved and trusted. Because of the deep trauma involved, there is often a long period of repressed feelings. When these feelings do break out and begin to express themselves, it creates an upheaval in the emotional and spiritual life of the person. Prayer becomes difficult. Why did God allow this to happen, and why did God also abandon them in the situation?

Jesus' heart-cry of abandonment on the cross "My God, my God, why have you forsaken me?" encourages you to speak what is often left unspoken. When you acknowledge and express the pain of rejection or loneliness in the heart, healing can begin. A heart deeply scarred by the wounds of abandonment needs to cry aloud.

God hears the heart-cry of abandonment, victimization, and loneliness. King David offered up his pain and declared, "A broken and contrite heart, O God, you will not despise" (Ps. 51:17).

6

Prayer as Jubilation

Jubilation is a word that sounds like what it means. It explodes out of the mouth with breath and energy. It means the expression of great joy. It can refer either to the act of exalting another, or to the lifting up of your own mind or spirit.

When applied to prayer, jubilation can relate to both meanings. Jubilant prayer does involve the exaltation of God, proclaiming the honor and glory that belongs to God, but it also describes the state of the pray-er when such prayer is offered. In exalting God your own spirit is lifted up in joy and gratitude.

Jubilation is the interaction between exalting God and experiencing within yourself the uplifting of your spirit. Both of these are important in the experience of prayer. The motive in jubilation is acknowledging God. One of the effects is to experience joy within yourself.

The Christian's experience of joy is not generated from within oneself or dependent on outer circumstances, because the source of joy is God. Knowing God and experiencing God's presence brings joy to your life. Theologian Teilhard de Chardin said, "Joy is the infallible sign of God's presence." Joy is listed as one of the effects of the Holy Spirit's presence in the life of the Christian in Galatians: "By contrast, the fruit of the Spirit is love, joy . . ." (Gal. 5:22).

The experience of feeling good can come from many sources. Compliments make you feel good. Success makes you feel good.

Having your life in balance makes you feel good. But many things in life can also cause you to feel bad. Both good and bad feelings are emotional responses to life situations. Your inner disposition can affect your emotions as well and make you feel up or down.

Joy as part of the fruit of the Spirit is not limited to emotional response or inner disposition. Rather, it is related to knowledge and faith as well as to feeling. Knowing who God is and believing in the steadfast love of God for your life is the foundation of this type of joy. When you immerse yourself in this knowledge and trust, the exaltation of God flows from you and in turn elevates your mind and spirit.

Prayers of jubilation are made up of two types of prayer—praise and thanksgiving. Praise is the prayer that exalts God for being God. Thanksgiving is the prayer that exalts God for what God has done or given. The one focuses on adoration of the being of God. The other prayer is gratitude for the action of God.

Prayer as Praise

Praise is a facet of faith. Belief in God as the Creator and Redeemer of your life will bring you to the act of praise and adoration. Awareness of the personal, living God who made you and loved you so much that he sent his Son to die for you will cause you to praise. The awe you experience in seeing the Creator of all mixes with the wonder at the Redeemer's love. The result is a prayer of praise filled with amazement that such a God exists. You are known by God and loved by God. Could there ever be a better reason to exalt and glorify the name of God?

I am often amazed watching people leave a worship service with their eyes downcast, their mouths turned down, and a scowl on their faces. God's word has been shared, God's glorious deeds displayed and love expressed in a personal way, and yet the spirit of praise was not expressed. Joy was not evident in their faces or manner. It may be that praise has not been a part of their prayer experience or the fruits of praise in their expectations. It may be that their inner eyes are focused on those things that have led them to the down side of life. It is possible to become so pre-occupied with problems relating to economics, relationships, addictions, or past mistakes that the glory and wonder of God are not visible.

Praise flows from a vision of the glory and majesty of God. Praise emerges from the experience of God's overwhelming love and grace in Christ Jesus. Praise erupts at the realization of the indwelling Spirit of God. That is the reason that so often you find in the Scripture the admonition to praise preceded by an accounting of God's creative power and compassionate love:

We ponder your steadfast love, O God,
    in the midst of your temple.
Your name, O God, like your praise,
    reaches to the ends of the earth. (Ps. 48:9-10)

Praise the Lord!
Praise God in his sanctuary;
    praise him in his mighty firmament!
Praise him for his mighty deeds;
    praise him according to his surpassing greatness! (Ps. 150:1-2)

Prayers of praise will arise from remembering who God is. In the midst of all that is petty, mean, low-spirited, and depressing in the world, the memory of God will lead you to the place of praise. In praising you will be lifted above that environment to taste the joy of the Lord once again.

The psalmist David wrote in the midst of the wilderness while he was being hunted down to be killed. You would almost expect a total lament from him. However, he wrote:

O God, you are my God, I seek you,
    my soul thirsts for you;
my flesh faints for you,
    as in a dry and weary land where there is no water.
So I have looked upon you in the sanctuary,
    beholding your power and glory.
Because your steadfast love is better than life,
    my lips will praise you.
So I will bless you as long as I live;
    I will lift up my hands and call on your name.
My soul is satisfied as with a rich feast,
    and my mouth praises you with joyful lips
when I think of you on my bed,

and meditate on you in the watches of the night;
for you have been my help,
and in the shadow of your wings I sing for joy.
(Ps. 63:1-7)

This experience is echoed in the New Testament in the journeys of the apostle Paul. In Philippi he and Barnabas are thrown into prison. In the middle of the night they are up praying and singing hymns. An earthquake frees them from prison.

Time and time again Christians have discovered that if they will remember who God is in power and love and if they offer praise, exalting God, a change will occur. Praise will lift their vision and spirits and set them on the Rock that is higher than they are.

God is worthy of praise. God never demands praise yet receives it as people realize the personal existence of the Creator and Jesus Christ.

It is interesting to note that one of the temptations of Jesus in the wilderness was for him to bow down and adore the devil. The devil was seeking from Jesus that which he did not deserve or have title to—adoration and praise. They alone belong to God.

When you consistently and eagerly offer praise in prayer to God you are not allowing yourself to be tempted to adore something or someone else in God's place. You can make prayers of praise a part of each day's devotion so that God remains the only one worthy to receive your praise.

Praise is also an antidote to pride. It is possible to fall into the habit of using God as something of an errand person. You keep God in the anteroom to call on whenever you need something. You begin to hold on to the reins of your life and soon elevate yourself to the top position. Praise will soon become difficult and something you will avoid if pride gains so much power in your life.

The Book of Revelation contains a wonderful image of God's creatures offering praise. The scene is the throne room and God is seated on the throne. Around the throne are four living creatures and twenty-four elders. They sing back and forth. The four living creatures sing, "Holy, Holy, Holy, the Lord God the Almighty, who was and is and is to come." The twenty-four elders respond with, "You are worthy, our Lord and God, to receive glory and honor and power, for you created all things, and by your will they existed and were created" (Rev. 4:8,11). Later the image grows larger:

> Then I looked, and I heard the voice of many angels surrounding the throne and the living creatures and the elders; they numbered myriads of myriads and thousands of thousands, singing with full voice, "Worthy is the Lamb that was slaughtered to receive power and wealth and wisdom and might and honor and glory and blessing!" Then I heard every creature in heaven and on earth and under the earth and in the sea, and all that is in them, singing, "To the one seated on the throne and to the Lamb be blessing and honor and glory and might forever and ever!" (Rev. 5:11-13)

These visions in Revelation are wonderful reminders of the need for and joy of praise. All things and beings have come from God and return to God. All things are made to praise their Maker, and this praise will be endless. A mark of our commitment to God in Jesus Christ is praise. As creatures of God with all the rest of creation we are called upon to bear witness to God's worthiness to be praised.

As with all types of prayer, praise is to be practiced. An experiment you could try is to test the value of praise in your own life.

Make a commitment to pray specifically a prayer of praise each morning and evening for thirty days. Do not be motivated by how you are feeling on any particular day. Each day focus on a particular attribute of God or experience of God's presence or action of God relative to your own life. Praise God for that. Remember that praise means to elevate, lift up, or exalt. Give expression to your sense of adoration for your Maker and Redeemer. Remember your own experiences of the way in which God has been gracious to you. The language of praise is alleluia, blessing, honor, glory, beauty, and holiness. In the beginning you may find it difficult to sustain a prayer of praise. As you reflect on who God is, letting that move through you, you may find yourself being able to extend your prayer of praise. Songs and psalms may also be praise expressions you would want to use. After a few days of this experiment, begin to see how the discipline of praise is affecting your attitudes, emotions, thinking, and relationships. Notice whether or not you are more conscious of God's presence than before. You may want to read Philippians 4:4 before each exercise of praise as an encouragement: "Rejoice in the Lord always; again I will say, Rejoice."

Prayer as Thanksgiving

A companion to the prayer of praise is the prayer of thanksgiving. Like the prayer of praise, thanksgiving begins with an inner awareness and attitude. This awareness is summarized in the Letter of James: "Every generous act of giving, with every perfect gift, is from above, coming down from the Father of lights, with whom there is no variation or shadow due to change" (James 1:17).

Everything you have is a gift from God. Underlying all the ways in which your life has been blessed with food, clothing, family, friends, nature, work, play, and things is the hand of God. All spiritual, material, social, and mental reality has come into being through God's creative power. "In him we live and move and have our being" (Acts 17:28).

The Christian community has always understood and confessed that God is the Creator of all and that all things exist in God. If you consciously live with this awareness, gratitude becomes an automatic response. However, as humans we are not without our struggle at this point. It is difficult to remember this and express thanksgiving at all times.

More and more of the world around us bears the mark of human creativity rather than God's. Through food processing and the changing of the environment it seems as if all that we have is a product of human ingenuity. This is especially true in urban environments. We do not have the daily reminders of the natural process of planting and harvesting. Animals, forest, plains, and beautiful wild streams are not something we encounter daily.

Add to this the natural human tendency to take ownership of what is in reach, and you have the makings of a person who may find it difficult to be aware that God is behind all that exists.

The beginning of a deep awareness of God's role in creating and sustaining life often comes through a spiritual awakening as

God becomes real in a saving, healing, or redeeming way. As the good news of Jesus Christ takes root in a person's life, he or she will begin a journey to learn the meaning of giving thanks. As more and more of life becomes touched by an awakened faith, God's relationship to all aspects of life will gradually become clear. Gratitude to God may become extended to more and more areas of life. Soon, with the growth of the Spirit, the Christian discovers that there is nothing but that which God has provided.

However, that scenario is not as simple as it sounds. Every Christian, no matter how mature, struggles with maintaining an attitude of gratitude. A friend of mine who is a mature and aware Christian told me the story of a day he had a rude awakening. He was lying on an air mattress on the lake where he had his cabin. He looked at the tall pines on the shore and the blue sky above with a few puffs of clouds. He noticed the family of ducks swimming by. He began to reminisce about how far he had come from his boyhood poverty. In a moment of exaltation he cried out, "Mine! All mine!" Then, in a moment of repentance he said, "O God, forgive me. It is yours! All yours!"

Just as we need to be diligent in praising God daily, we need to exercise thanksgiving in all things.

Remembering the specific ways in which God has blessed your life and giving thanks each day is a discipline that is important to maintain. It will keep your relationship with God vital and alive. It will lead you to be less anxious about your life and to recognize that God does take care of you. It will help free you to be able to give to others as God has given to you.

Prayers of thanksgiving to God may seem easy when many blessings are flowing to you, but there are those difficult times. Tragedy strikes. Jobs are lost. Sickness prevails. Families are torn apart. Abusive memories haunt. How do you pray then?

The New Testament teaching on prayer includes encouragement to pray with thanksgiving in all circumstances in life. Through both direct admonition and examples of early Christians, the New Testament teaches that Christians are to pray with thanksgiving in even the worst of circumstances.

1 Thessalonians 5:18 is very direct in the admonition to pray with thanksgiving: "Give thanks in all circumstances; for this is

the will of God in Christ Jesus for you." This teaching is echoed in several other New Testament books:

And whatever you do, in word or deed, do everything in the name of the Lord Jesus, giving thanks to God the Father through him. (Col. 3:17)

Do not worry about anything, but in everything by prayer and supplication with thanksgiving let your requests be made known to God. (Phil. 4:6)

By giving thanks in all circumstances you witness that you trust God to act in all situations. This is not to say that God creates our troubles, tragedies, or trials. It does say that God can and will act in the midst of them to create good out of them. These passages about giving thanks in all circumstances can be linked to Romans 8:28: "We know that all things work together for good for those who love God, who are called according to his purpose."

Prayers of thanksgiving in difficult circumstances do give witness to trust in God's desire and ability to act on our behalf.

If you pray a prayer of thanksgiving in the midst of a tragedy, it will help turn your attention to God, and then you can begin to look with hope for what God might do to redeem and transform the experience.

You have probably experienced the fact that anxiety, anger, or vengeance have not brought transformation to life's situations. Even though these feelings are natural and will be experienced, you can begin to discipline yourself to respond to all situations with thanksgiving and move beyond paralyzing or destructive emotions.

The writer of Psalm 92 says it best: "It is good to give thanks to the Lord, to sing praises to your name, O Most High; to declare your steadfast love in the morning, and your faithfulness by night" (vv. 1-2).

It is good to give thanks to the Lord. It is good to give thanks because that is what God expects from his children. God who freely gives out of grace and in abundance looks for the grateful heart to respond. It is also good to give thanks because it keeps our spiritual life in balance. It delivers us from anxiety or acting on destructive feelings. Thanksgiving keeps us focused on God's redeeming and transforming possibilities for every situation.

As in other forms of prayer, we see that thanksgiving is a vital discipline in maintaining a healthy relationship with God and in our own spirituality.

You may want to develop a pattern or discipline in your own life so that prayers of thanksgiving become a part of your daily routine—giving thanks before each meal; thanking God upon awakening; naming and thanking God each evening for the blessings of the day, and consciously linking each event and person encountered in the day to the ongoing presence of Christ in your life.

Forging a habit of gratitude in these obvious situations of blessing and goodness will prepare you to be able to give thanks in the difficult circumstances.

7

Suggestions for Prayer Disciplines

The following suggestions are offered to assist you in developing prayer disciplines and experiences that will open more options for your prayer life. Practice a wide variety of prayer patterns so that you will more fully discover the methods of prayer that best fit you and will allow you to follow where your heart and mind lead in responding to God. These suggestions may help you discover certain methods of your own that will be fulfilling for you.

An Acronym Reminder for Prayer

A Adoration: praising God
C Confession: acknowledging your sins and struggles
T Thanksgiving: naming your blessings and thanking God for them
S Supplications: offering up your requests for yourself and others.

Biblical Reflection

- Center yourself through silence, allowing your cares and concerns to move aside.

- Read slowly a portion of Scripture. Notice each word and image.
- Choose a phrase or image in the Scripture that seems to catch your attention. Fix it firmly in your mind.
- Reflect on what you have chosen. Let it speak to you and your life.
- After reflecting, form a prayer of response and pray that prayer.
- Journal, write down, any significant thoughts and your prayer response.

Prayer List

Purchase a notebook that will become your prayer journal. Designate a page for your prayer list. On this list keep a record of the persons, situations, and needs for which you would like to pray daily. At first you may be inclined to put every situation and person you encounter on that list. However, you will find that your list will grow beyond the amount of time you have to pray. Be selective in what you put on your prayer list. God calls each of us to take on certain prayer burdens. Seek God's direction in choosing whom and for what you ought to pray in an ongoing way. You are free to pray for anyone and anything at any given moment. However, you will find yourself drawn to certain needs to which you will want to commit yourself over a longer period of time.

Set apart a specific time to use your prayer list. Each day go through your list in intercessions for those items you have written down. You may want to keep a record in the rest of the notebook of answered prayers as you become aware of them. This is an encouraging practice as you continue to see how God answers the prayers of his people.

Learning to Pray in a Group

Verbally praying in a group is difficult for some people. This can be true even in a family circle gathering. Often the reason is simply that one has not done it before. An easy method of gaining experience in this practice is to gather with a group and go through the following pattern. First, each person will share a concern for which he or she would like prayer. It may be personal or relate to someone else. Each person around the circle, in turn, will share in this way. Next, go around the circle again, only this time each person will pray a brief one-sentence prayer for the concern named by the person on his or her right. The use of this method will encourage listening and enable people to become comfortable praying out loud in a group. An alternative to this is the practice of having each person respond with a sentence prayer immediately after the person on their left has shared a concern.

Praying with the Psalms

The Book of Psalms has been the primary prayer book of the Jews and Christians for many centuries. It covers the full range of human experience and expression of human need. Developing a daily discipline of reading the psalms will become a rich learning experience in the school of prayer. Read the psalm or a portion of it aloud. Reflect on it, seeking to capture the spirit of the prayer that is in it. Let these thoughts lead you to a prayer that reflects the same spirit of the psalm in relation to specific things in your own life. (See also page 96.)

Morning and Evening Prayer

A prayer discipline that many people use is to frame the day with prayer. On rising, offer a prayer of praise and acknowledgment of God. Then, as you think through what the day will bring, pray for each specific concern that you have for it. At the close of the day, give thanks for all the blessings that have come. Ask forgiveness for any resentments, sins, or other negative experiences.

The Jesus Prayer

A prayer form that developed out of a search to discover what it meant to "pray without ceasing" is called the "Jesus Prayer."

It is a combination of centering on your breathing and repeating the phrase "Lord Jesus Christ, Son of God, have mercy on me, a sinner." You begin by positioning your body in a relaxed but attentive position. Then, focus on the above phrase or a shorter version of it, such as "Lord Jesus, have mercy," or just the word "Jesus." The words follow your breath. As you breathe in, say, "Lord Jesus Christ, Son of God." As you exhale, say the words, "Have mercy on me, a sinner." Continue this for a period of time, letting the words follow your breathing pattern. Let your breathing remain natural and unforced. Do not try to establish a breathing pattern. Try to keep focused on what you are saying and allow the words to maintain a steady rhythm of following your breath. This prayer will bring a great sense of peace and often a sense of God's presence. Some who have practiced this prayer will find themselves waking up in the morning with this prayer going on within them. It is as if you are establishing an ongoing prayer with your breath.

A Prayer Walk or Run

Many people find that prayer becomes easier or more natural when they are moving or out-of-doors. The rhythm of running or walking with the surrounding beauty of nature is a context in which prayer may flow more easily and provide a deeper sense of God's presence. You can set out on such a walk or run with the express purpose of focusing on a conversation with God.

Moments with God

If your life is extremely busy and you find it difficult to establish a regular, long period of time for developing your prayer discipline, plan to spend a certain number of briefer moments in prayer in a regular daily pattern. You can set apart three, five, or seven times a day when you would pray from three to five minutes. Such a pattern could include rising, morning coffee, lunch, late afternoon, and evening. You could combine this with reflection on a single Bible verse chosen for each of these prayer times. This is similar to the monastic practice of alternating work, leisure, and prayer throughout the day.

Devotional Aids

Your prayer discipline can be strengthened by providing various devotional aids for your prayer time. An icon, candle, cross, or other religious symbols can be used to create a worship center in your home. A designated chair may become your prayer place. A poster, favorite picture, or Scripture passages can be hung near your prayer place. A hymn book, Bible, and other resources for prayer can be kept nearby.

These preparations in creating a place for your regular prayer time will help to sustain an ongoing discipline.

8

Learning to Pray from Others

The Christian community is a praying community and a place where you learn from and are sustained by others. The gift and art of prayer have been at the center of this community from the beginning. From the prayers of others you can learn much that will assist you in finding ways to make prayer a central part of your life. Let yourself be teachable as you journey in prayer.

Learning from the Psalms

This ancient prayer book has accompanied the people of God for centuries. Each generation has found the psalms to be a rich source of learning about prayer. As you read and pray these psalms, you will find them speaking about your own life in all its parts, moods, and circumstances.

The psalms will encourage you to be open and honest before God. They are filled with questions about life, God, and oneself. These questions grew out of the life experience of the psalmists as they sought to understand their life situations in the light of God's love and goodness. Notice the openness and intensity of feeling expressed in these questions found in the psalms:

O God, why do you cast us off forever?

Why does your anger smoke against the sheep of your
pasture? (Ps. 74:1)

My God, my God, why have you forsaken me?
    Why are you so far from helping me, from the words of
my groaning? (Ps. 22:1)

How long, O Lord? Will you forget me forever?
    How long will you hide your face from me?
How long must I bear pain in my soul,
    and have sorrow in my heart all day long? (Ps. 13:1-2)

Why, O Lord, do you stand far off?
    Why do you hide yourself in times of trouble? (Ps. 10:1)

The psalmists were not afraid to express their feelings openly
to God. They did not hide their frustration, anger, fear, or shame.
You may be tempted not to allow all your feelings to enter your
prayer life. This may come from a false notion that only "nice"
things are to be said to God. God knows our life. God knows our
feelings. God is not put off by honesty. In fact, the thing that
God desires is truth and sincerity.

Whether it is the serene, pastoral images of Psalm 23 expressing
a calm confidence in God's care, or Psalm 137 with its cry for
vengeance, prayer is meant to express our true feelings and responses to our life situations.

Truth and sincerity apply to positive as well as to negative
emotions. Notice the straightforward expression of confidence
and unbridled joy in these psalm verses:

Vindicate me, O Lord,
    for I have walked in my integrity,
    and I have trusted in the Lord without wavering.
Prove me, O Lord, and try me;
    test my heart and mind.
For your steadfast love is before my eyes,
    and I walk in faithfulness to you. (Ps. 26:1-3)

O come, let us sing to the Lord;
    let us make a joyful noise to the rock of our salvation!
(Ps. 95:1)

In the prayer conversation with God the psalms will also teach
you about the inner dialogue with your soul. These prayers plumb

the depths of the inner journey of prayer. The psalmist's conscious mind speaks to the deeper reality of the soul and calls it into conversation with God:

Why are you cast down, O my soul,
    and why are you disquieted within me?
Hope in God; for I shall again praise him,
    my help and my God. (Ps. 42:5)

Bless the Lord, O my soul,
    and all that is within me,
    bless his holy name. (Ps. 103:1)

As modern people many Christians find it difficult to define the soul or to talk about it meaningfully. An emphasis on rationalism and materialism has tended to discount the reality of the nonmaterial and spiritual. A careful reading and reflection on the psalms may help to restore confidence in the reality of inner, spiritual experience that will allow your prayer life to blossom fully. The psalms do not discredit the material and rational. These aspects of life are fully present in these prayers. However, they also give full expression to the deep soul experience in relating to God.

From the psalms you can also learn about the relationship between prayer and the deep healing of your life. Many of the psalms are prayers of confession and describe the healing experienced when sin is acknowledged and God's mercy is received. Notice in Psalm 32 how the agony and pain of unconfessed sin is relieved when the psalmist confesses:

Happy are those whose transgression is forgiven,
    whose sin is covered. . . .
While I kept silence, my body wasted away
    through my groaning all day long.
For day and night your hand was heavy upon me;
    my strength was dried up as by the heat of summer.
Then I acknowledged my sin to you,
    and I did not hide my iniquity;
I said, "I will confess my transgressions to the Lord,"
    and you forgave the guilt of my sin. (Ps. 32:1,3-5)

In Psalm 51 King David prays a beautiful prayer of confession, seeking healing in the deep places of his life. Notice how he realizes that his sin is deep within him and how necessary it is that God cleanse him and restore him:

> Against you, you alone, have I sinned,
>   and done what is evil in your sight,
> so that you are justified in your sentence
>   and blameless when you pass judgment.
> Indeed I was born guilty,
>   a sinner when my mother conceived me.
> You desire truth in the inward being;
>   therefore teach me wisdom in my secret heart.
> Purge me with hyssop, and I shall be clean;
>   wash me, and I shall be whiter than snow.
> Let me hear joy and gladness;
>   let the bones that you have crushed rejoice. (Ps. 51:4-8)

The deepest need any of us has is for this type of healing in our lives. The guilt, shame, and fear that flow from sin carry such destructive power. Sharing our whole lives with God opens the door for God's grace and mercy to transform us and to restore our wholeness and balance. The psalms point the way for us to pray with complete honesty and humility, trusting with great confidence in the mercy and forgiving love of God. The New Testament fulfills and completes this truth with the gift of the Savior, Jesus. The honesty of the psalms combined with the gift of the clear love of God displayed in the cross of Christ is an avenue of prayer that can give the deep healing we all need.

Another lesson from the psalms is the encouragement they give to pray in trust and confidence. The psalmists continuously affirm in their prayers the steadfast love and faithfulness of God. They never tire of reciting the marvelous works of God in their history and the fact that God can be trusted to act now. In learning to pray in faith, imitate the psalms by including in your prayers the remembrance of God's mighty deeds. As your prayer grows from these remembrances, you will be encouraged to pray out of faith and not out of the despair at what surrounds you in the world.

Distinguishing between faith and feelings is a difficult task. They seem to lie side by side within us. Our feelings can often

99

be so strong that they totally dominate our attention and dictate our responses to life. Faith, however, is not just a response to feelings; it is chiefly an act of the will and mind to affirm trust in God's faithfulness and steadfast love.

Notice the wonderful way in which the psalmists include praise and adoration in their prayers and confidently affirm God's desire to help and to save:

O give thanks to the Lord, for he is good;
for his steadfast love endures forever. (Ps. 107:1)

O sing to the Lord a new song,
for he has done marvelous things.
His right hand and his holy arm
have gotten him victory. (Ps. 98:1)

O Lord my God, I cried to you for help,
and you have healed me. (Ps. 30:2)

O Lord, you will hear the desire of the meek;
you will strengthen their heart, you will incline your ear
to do justice for the orphan and the oppressed,
so that those from earth may strike terror no more.
(Ps. 10:17-18)

One of the strongest lessons the psalms can teach you has to do with the way you see. For the psalmists, God is everywhere. There is no gift but what comes from God. There is no life but what comes from God. There is no rescue but what comes from God. There is no food but what comes from God. This way of seeing undergirds the marvelous prayers in the book of Psalms. It is a vision toward which prayer should move. As your prayer life deepens, God will become more and more present to each moment of your life and more visible in all the signs of life around you. Each moment will carry a metaphor or symbol that can give life and vitality to your conversation with God. Spend some time meditating on Psalm 104 as an example of how you can begin to see God's footprints and sense God's presence in all of life.

Do not neglect the psalms as a teacher and companion on your prayer journey.

Learning from the Lord's Prayer

In response to his disciples' request to teach them to pray, Jesus gave them the prayer we call the Lord's Prayer. It is a brief but powerful example of prayer that can help us to understand how to pray. Some Christians use this prayer several times a day, letting it become the model prayer for their devotional expression to God. It is worth your time to explore this prayer by meditating on its petitions and letting it become a daily discipline of frequent use.

Our Father in heaven,
  hallowed be your name,
  your kingdom come,
  your will be done,
    on earth as in heaven.
Give us today our daily bread.
Forgive us our sins
  as we forgive those
    who sin against us.
Save us from the time of trial
  and deliver us from evil.
For the kingdom, the power,
  and the glory are yours,
  now and forever. Amen

Our Father, who art in heaven,
  hallowed be thy name,
  thy kingdom come,
  thy will be done,
    on earth as it is in heaven.
Give us this day our daily bread;
and forgive us our trespasses,
  as we forgive those
    who trespass against us;
and lead us not into temptation,
  but deliver us from evil.
For thine is the kingdom,
  and the power, and the glory,
  forever and ever. Amen

Since the Lord's Prayer was given by Jesus, it has a special place in most Christian communities. It is a prayer that will reside deep within your soul and be a vital link to a sense, whether conscious or unconscious, of God's presence in your life.

On one occasion I was called to the hospital to minister to an elderly person who was dying. She was in a coma when I arrived and had been unresponsive to the communication of family and nursing staff. I spoke to the woman about God's redemptive love in Jesus and prayed for her. Then I began praying the Lord's Prayer. By the third sentence of the prayer I noticed her lips moving in unison with the words I was saying. Even though she made no sound, from deep within, where the prayer had become implanted in her soul, she was responding and participating in this conversation with God.

It is wonderful to have the truth of this prayer planted deep within us. It can provide an unconscious yet real and ongoing prayer life that continues, even when the conscious mind is asleep.

The Lord's Prayer is a good teacher about prayer because it is so simple and direct. It acknowledges God as One beyond us and yet as a tender-hearted and compassionate Father. It further praises God by holding up the holiness of God's name. God's kingdom, that is, God's rule and will in our world, is requested. There follow three very basic needs in our life—daily food, receiving and giving forgiveness, and protection from evil.

This fundamental prayer teaches us to honor God, open our lives to God's will, live without anxiety and fear by trusting God for our daily needs, exercising forgiveness, and knowing we are protected from evil.

Learning from Classic Prayers

In the Christian community we learn from each other. The wealth of wisdom from Christians past and present is a continuous source of learning and encouragement. This is true of prayer as well as other aspects of our religious life.

You can gain inspiration and insight from the prayers handed down through the centuries. These prayers have been a wellspring of encouragement and teaching for the spiritual lives and prayer journeys of Christians all over the world. Often they provide ways of praying with creativity and sensitivity when our own well is dry and our spirit is lagging.

You may find it helpful to use these prayers as a way to find your own voice in prayer. The creativity of style and the wisdom of the content can be a teacher for your own prayer journey with God.

The following are classics of prayer that have fed countless numbers of people with their inspiration and ability to touch the human situation in which we all find ourselves.

God grant me the serenity
To accept the things that I cannot change,
The courage to change the things I can,

And the wisdom to know the difference.
    (Reinhold Niebuhr)

Most merciful Redeemer, Friend and Brother, may we know
Thee more clearly, love Thee more dearly, and follow Thee
more nearly: for Thine own sake. Amen.
    (Richard of Chichester)

God, give us grateful hearts.
For if we do not have the grace to thank Thee for all
that we have and enjoy, how can we have the effrontery to
seek Thy further blessing?
For Jesus' sake. Amen.
    (Peter Marshall)[4]

Thou hast given so much to me,
Give one thing more—a grateful heart;
Not thankful when it pleases me,
As if Thy blessings had spare days,
But such a heart whose pulse may be
Thy praise.
    (George Herbert)[5]

O Lord, the sea is so large and my boat is so small.
Have mercy and help me. Amen.
    (Celtic Prayer)

Come, Holy Spirit, fill the hearts of your faithful, and kindle
in us the fire of your love. Send forth your Spirit and we
shall be created and you shall renew the face of the earth.
O God, who by the light of your Holy Spirit did instruct the
hearts of the faithful, grant that by that same Spirit we may
be truly wise and ever enjoy his consolations. Through Christ
our Lord. Amen.
    (Adapted from the Psalms and ancient collects)

Learning from Hymns and Liturgy

Most hymns are prayers set to music. They express praise,
thanksgiving, desire, and grief. These poems are another source
of learning about prayer. Augustine said, "To sing is to pray

103

twice." Combining music and poetry involves more dimensions of yourself in the act of praying. Music helps to draw out the emotions of the heart and lets our thoughts, body, and feelings join together in prayer.

Begin to think of your hymn and spiritual song singing as an act of prayer, whether you sing alone or with others. Discover how your singing changes when you think of it as prayer. Forget what your voice may sound like and let your whole self join in this prayer experience. God is interested that you pray and not so much in how you sound when you pray. God is listening to the heart-cry of your prayer, not to the quality of your voice.

The liturgy of your church can function in the same way. It gives one voice to the people of God gathered for prayer. However, the language and song of the liturgy can also be the prayer of one voice. These ancient and abiding prayers of the church can become the vehicle for a rich prayer life, whether alone or with others.

The Kyrie, "Lord, have mercy," is the church's cry for help from God for those places where things are out of control and beyond our capacity to change. The Gloria, "Glory to God in the highest," is the prayer of strong confidence that rises from the church that God can and will respond as God has done in the past, especially in the person of Jesus Christ.

These and other portions of the liturgy can become your personal prayer forms as well as the prayer of the gathered congregation. By using them yourself you gain a sense of solidarity with the whole faith community.

When my wife and I paddle our canoe in the early morning hours of the northern wilderness, we often quietly sing the liturgy of the church as our morning prayer. It gathers the whole host of believers around us in the midst of God's wondrous creation as we worship.

You are not alone in your prayer journey. Thousands have journeyed before and thousands journey with you today. Enrich your prayer life from the collected wisdom and devotion of your brothers and sisters in the faith. Scriptures, hymns, liturgy, the prayers of others—all these are resources that will assist you in learning to pray.

9

Prayer and Life's Journey

Your prayer life may have begun when as a small child you spoke these words as you went to bed:

Now I lay me down to sleep.
I pray the Lord my soul to keep.
If I should die before I wake,
I pray the Lord my soul to take.

And at the end of life, the prayer often echoes Jesus' last words on the cross: "Father, into your hands I commend my spirit."

Moving full circle from birth to death, life is enfolded with the knowledge and the prayer of receiving life as a gift and offering it back to God.

In between these simple bookends of prayer, life is filled with the struggle to know yourself, others, and God, and with all the decisions that grow out of this knowledge. What should I do with my life? What is important and of value? With whom should I live my life?

You encounter change along life's journey from childhood to youth, to young adulthood, to mid-life, to older adulthood. Each change brings new experiences and challenges. Life is like a school that continually tests you through new tasks. Each stage brings a challenge to your faith, character, hope, strength, and love. You will encounter great joy and great sorrow, success and failure, love and rejection.

In, with, and under this journey is the ongoing presence of your Lord. God is there in the midst of all that life brings to you. Prayer is the opportunity to relate your life journey to that ever present reality of God's promise to love you and keep you forever.

For this reason, the ultimate test is to remain faithful to God as God has promised to be faithful to you. Your faithfulness can be nurtured through your commitment to pray so that your successes can be met with humility and your disappointments with hope.

Prayer will help you live with the knowledge that God has bread enough for the journey. God is present to each day with what it takes to nourish and sustain your life. The well of God's abundant grace never runs dry.

Prayer is not a journey of self-actualization in which you realize that you don't need God. Rather, prayer is a journey of discovery that you are being held in the palm of God's hand at every stage of life.

A commitment to the discipline of prayer within yourself and with others will keep you close to God's saving and nurturing grace in Christ Jesus. As the apostle Paul heard from the Lord "My grace is sufficient for you," so you can depend on that promise for your life.

I offer you the following thoughts as a summary that may help keep you in a healthy discipline of prayer:

- Seek God first in all things. Remember that the foundation for prayer is the relationship you have with God.
- Maintain a regular discipline of prayer. Find the way that is best for you to keep prayer at the center of your religious life. "Commit your way to the Lord; trust in him, and he will act" (Ps. 37:5).
- Pray, trusting in God's love for you. Center your prayer in the cross and resurrection of Jesus, where God has displayed that wondrous love for you.
- Give thanks in everything. Learn the power of gratitude and praise to transform your responses to life's situations.
- Follow God's lead in prayer. The Holy Spirit is the great teacher of prayer. Learn to discern the inner movement of God's Spirit in your soul.

- Expect to grow spiritually through your prayer discipline. Maturity will come in the enlightenment and wisdom God will bring to your life.
- Expect to be surprised. God, at times, will do more than you expect or can imagine.
- Offer God everything. Whatever you hold back for your own control can become a barrier to clarity in discerning God's will.
- Be honest in sharing with God.
- Listen, listen, listen.

All of life and all of prayer is a journey of return to the One who has made you, the One who waits eagerly for you with these words of invitation:

I am the Alpha and the Omega, the beginning and the end. To the thirsty I will give water as a gift from the spring of the water of life. Those who conquer will inherit these things, and I will be their God and they will be my children. (Rev. 21:6-7)

"Now I lay me down to sleep" and "Father, into your hands I commend my spirit," and all the prayers in between, are part of this marvelous journey with God that ends in God.

Notes

1. Henri J. Nouwen, *With Open Hands*, (Notre Dame, Ind.: Ave Maria Press, 1972), p. 12.
2. Clarence A. Johnson, "Open Mine Eyes, O Lord."
3. Dietrich Bonhoeffer, *Life Together* (New York: Harper and Row), p. 79.
4. Donald Kauffman, ed., *A Treasury of Great Prayers* (Westwood, N.J.: Fleming H. Revell, 1964), p. 23.
5. Ibid., p. 41.

For Further Reading

Anonymous. *The Cloud of Unknowing*. New York: Image Books, 1973.

Bloom, Anthony. *Beginning to Pray*. New York: Paulist Press, 1979.

Brother Lawrence. *The Practice of the Presence of God*. Old Tappen, N.J.: Revell, 1958.

Egan, Harvey D. *Christian Mysticism*. New York: Pueblo, 1984.

Foster, Richard J. *Prayer*. San Francisco: Harper, 1992.

Hallesby, O. *Prayer*. Minneapolis: Augsburg Books, 1993 (1931).

Kelsey, Morton T. *The Other Side of Silence*. New York: Paulist Press, 1976.

Michael, Chester D., and Marie C. Norrisey. *Prayer and Temperament*. Charlottesville, Va: The Open Door Inc., 1984.

Pennington, M. Basil. *Centering Prayer*. New York: Image Books, 1980.

Sager, Allan H. *Gospel-Centered Spirituality*. Minneapolis: Augsburg Books, 1990.

Teresa of Avila. *The Interior Castle*. New York: Paulist Press, 1979.